ABG Productions in association with Neil McPherson for the
Finborough Theatre presents

A Finborough Theatre commission

The European Premiere

RACHEL

by **Angelina Weld Grimké**

FINBOROUGH | THEATRE

First performed in the US in Washington D.C. in March 1916.
First performed at the Finborough Theatre: Tuesday, 30 September 2014.

RACHEL

by **Angelina Weld Grimké**

Cast in order of appearance

Mrs Loving	**Miquel Brown**
Rachel Loving	**Adelayo Adedayo**
Thomas Loving	**Nakay Kpaka**
Jimmy Mason	**Joel McDermott**
	or **William Wright-Neblett**
John Strong	**Zephryn Taitte**
Mrs Lane	**Sheila Atim**
Ethel Lane	**Kaylah Black**
	or **Lexyn Boahen**

The action takes place in a living room in the small apartment of Mrs Loving, in a northern city in the USA in the early years of the twentieth century.

Act I. October 16th.

Act II. October 16th, four years later

Act III. One week later.

The performance lasts approximately two hours

There will be one interval of fifteen minutes

Director	**Ola Ince**
Designer	**Alex Marker**
Lighting Designer	**Elliot Griggs**
Sound Designer	**Max Pappenheim**
Costume Designer	**Anna Lewis**
Casting Director	**Axa Hynes**
Stage Manager	**Shannon Martin**
Assistant Director	**Daniel Bailey**
Producers	**Aidan Grounds**
	Hannah Groombridge
	for **ABG Productions**

Our patrons are respectfully reminded that, in this intimate theatre, any noise such as rustling programmes, talking or the ringing of mobile phones may distract the actors and your fellow audience-members.

We regret there is no admittance or re-admittance to the auditorium whilst the performance is in progress.

Interval drinks may be ordered in advance from the bar.

Adelayo Adedayo | Rachel Loving
Trained at Identity.
Theatre includes *The Dead Wait* (Park Theatre).
Film includes *Jet Trash*, *London Fields*, *Gone Too Far* and *Sket*.
Television includes Viva in the BBC Three Comedy *Some Girls*, *Law and Order: UK*, *Skins*, *MI High*, *Meet the Bandaiis* and *The Bill*.

Sheila Atim | Mrs Lane
Trained at Weekend Arts College.
Theatre includes *The Lightning Child* (Globe Theatre), *Ghost Town (Tour for Pilot Theatre)* and *Klook's Last Stand* (Park Theatre).
Sheila is also a musician, songwriter and composer.

Miquel Brown | Mrs Loving
Trained at Ladre Ballet Academy, Seattle, and RADA.
Theatre includes *Dessa Rose* (Trafalgar Studios), *The Amen Corner* (National Theatre), *Reflection Day* (Theatre503), *Menopause – The Musical* (Shaw Theatre and National Tour), *Stamping Shouting and Singing Home* (Polka Theatre), *Stepping Out* (Theatre Royal Lincoln), *Showboat* (Royal Albert Hall), *A Streetcar Named Desire* (National Theatre Studio), *Purlie* (Bridewell Theatre), *Blues In the Night* (National Tour), *Mardi Gras* (Prince of Wales Theatre) and the original London cast of *Elegies for Angels, Punks and Raging Queens* (King's Head Theatre and Criterion Theatre).
Film includes *Woman In Gold*, *Locked In*, *How to Lose Friends and Alienate People*, *The Successor*, *An American Haunting*, *French Kiss*, *Superman* and *Soloman and Sheba*.
Television includes *9/11: The Twin Towers*, *Casualty* and *Wit*.

Nakay Kpaka | Tom Loving
Trained at Drama Centre.
Theatre includes *Othello* (Shakespeare's Globe).
Television includes *Broadchurch*, *Grantchester*, *Whitechapel* and *Headspace*.

Zephryn Taitte | John Strong
Theatre includes *The Man In The Green Jacket* (Jermyn Street Theatre), *The Jungle Book* (Birmingham Stage Company), *Sirens of Titan* (London Bubble Theatre), *The Island* (Rose Bruford College), *The Unfortunate Love of the British Empire* (Sketchbook), *The Tempest* (Ovalhouse), *The Crucible* (Talawa at the Drill Hall) and *Romeo and Juliet* (Ovalhouse).
Film includes *Dirty Money*, *The Tempest*, *Disorder*, *Dark Stranger*, *Flash Mob* and *187 Days*.
Television includes *Brothers with No Game* (Winner of Screen Nation's Digital-iS Favourite Actor Award 2013), *The Hour* and *60 Secs*.

Kaylah Black | Ethel Lane
Training at Sylvia Young Theatre School.
This is Kaylah's professional stage debut.

Lexyn Boahen | Ethel Lane
Training at Stagecoach Tooting and *The Lion King* Cub Camp.
Theatre includes *Peter Pan* (Wembley Arena), *Oliver!, Frozen, Little Shop of Horrors* and *Hairspray* (Stagecoach).

Joel McDermott | Jimmy Mason
Training at D&B Theatre School.
Theatre includes *Medea* (National Theatre).

William Wright-Neblett | Jimmy Mason
Training at the New London Performing Arts Centre and The Place Dance Centre.
Theatre includes *Messiah* (London Coliseum) and *The Lion King* (UK and Ireland tour).
Film includes *PAN*.
Television includes *Scaredycat* and *Little White Lies*.

Angelina Weld Grimké | Playwright

Angelina Weld Grimké (1880-1958) was a poet, dramatist, journalist, teacher, essayist, radical feminist and lesbian icon. She was born in Boston, Massachusetts, into a distinguished mixed-race family, which had included slaveholders and slaves, free black people, white abolitionists, and advocates for women's rights and women's suffrage. Her mother, Sarah E. Stanley, was white and worked as a scholar and a homemaker. Grimké's father, Archibald Henry Grimké, was a highly regarded attorney, diplomat, and scholar. He was only the second African-American to graduate from Harvard Law School. Grimké excelled academically – she published her first poem at age 13. Her earliest poems, published in Boston and in Washington, DC, focused on the realm of racial politics. Some critics feared that her words on prejudice were enough to cause violence in the streets and incite Blacks to rise up in the face of oppression. Despite this, Grimké remained personally introverted and dedicated to the quiet life of a teacher. During her summers, she took courses at Harvard, and in 1907, she became an English teacher at Washington's M Street High School. When she suffered back injuries in a 1911 train crash, Grimké became more isolated. Always sheltered, her new physical handicap led her to spend increasing amounts of time at her writing desk. Soon after the accident, she began work on a three-act play called *Rachel*.

The Drama Committee of the National Association for the Advancement of Colored People (NAACP) first produced *Rachel* in March 1916 in Washington, DC after a call for new works to rally public opinion against D. W. Griffith's recently released film, *The Birth of a Nation* (1915), which glorified the Ku Klux Klan and portrayed a racist view of blacks and of their role in the American Civil War and Reconstruction in the South. The play – one of the first to be performed by an all-black cast – was subsequently performed at the Neighborhood Playhouse, New York City, and in Cambridge, Massachusetts. *Rachel* earned Grimké considerable acclaim, and was published in 1920.

Analysis by modern literary critics has provided strong evidence that Grimké was lesbian or bisexual. Some critics believe this is expressed in her published poetry in a subtle way, but more evidence came after her death by scholars' study of her diaries and more explicit unpublished works. *The Dictionary of Literary Biography: African-American Writers Before the Harlem Renaissance* states: "In several poems and in her diaries Grimké expressed the frustration that her lesbianism created; thwarted longing is a theme in several poems." Some of her unpublished poems are more explicitly lesbian, implying that she lived a life of suppression, "both personal and creative."

She is widely regarded as a leading forerunner of the Harlem Renaissance, the cultural, social, and artistic explosion that took place in Harlem between the end of the First World War and the middle of the 1930s. Grimké's talents were much admired by the poets and writers of the Harlem Renaissance including Langston Hughes and Countee Cullen, who convinced Grimké to be published in a 1927 anthology entitled *Caroling Dusk*. After this, she spent the remainder of her life in quiet isolation. Grimké died on June 10 1958. Long after her death, Grimké's works returned to popularity. Despite her timid persona, she is now remembered as a lyrical and fearless chronicler of the personal and political dilemmas of her era.

Ola Ince | Director
Productions at the Finborough Theatre include the world premiere of Chris Dunkley's *The Soft of Her Palm* and May Sumbwanyambe's *Back Home Contemplation* as part of The Papatango New Writing Festival. Ola was formerly a Resident Assistant Director at the Finborough Theatre, assisting on *Fanta Orange* and *Blue Surge*.
Trained at Rose Bruford College in Theatre Directing.
Direction includes *Treading Air* (Bush Theatre), *HOT* (Invertigo at the Hightide Festival), *A Piece of Cake* (Tristan Bates Theatre), *Pets Corner* (Arcola Theatre), *One Million Tiny Plays About Britain* (The Clare Theatre at The Young Vic), and *Games* (Pleasance London). Assistant Direction includes *Porgy and Bess* (Open Air Theatre, Regent's Park), *A Taste of Honey* (National Theatre), *Josephine and I* (Bush Theatre), *Wild Swans* and *Disco Pigs* (The Young Vic) and *Secret Thoughts and The Demolition Man* (Octagon Theatre, Bolton).

Alex Marker | Designer
Alex has been Resident Designer of the Finborough Theatre since 2002 where he has designed 30 productions including: *Soldiers*, *Trelawny of the 'Wells'*, *Hortensia and the Museum of Dreams*, *Albert's Boy*, *Lark Rise to Candleford*, *Red Night*, *Eden's Empire*, *Little Madam*, *Plague Over England* and its West End transfer to the Duchess Theatre, *Hangover Square*, *Sons of York*, *Death of Long Pig*, *Molière or The League of Hypocrites*, *Dream of the Dog* and its West End transfer to the Trafalgar Studios, *Me and Juliet*, *Quality Street*, *Fanta Orange*, *Outward Bound*, *So Great a Crime*, *London Wall* and *The White Carnation* and its transfer to Jermyn Street Theatre. He has also directed at the Finborough Theatre including two staged readings as part of the Finborough Theatre's *Vibrant – A Festival of Finborough Playwrights* and sell-out revivals of William Douglas Home's *Portraits* and J.B. Priestley's *Summer Day's Dream*. Trained in Theatre Design at Wimbledon School of Art, he has designed over fifty productions including: *The Trial of Jane Fonda* (Assembly Rooms, Edinburgh), *Around the World in 80 Days* (Theatre Chipping Norton and Tour), *London Calling* (Salisbury Playhouse), *What the Women Did, The Moment of Truth* (Southwark Playhouse), *Tape* (Trafalgar Studios), *Frankie and Johnny in the Clair de Lune* (Chipping Norton), *Rift* (Brewhouse Theatre, Taunton), *Jus' Like That - An Evening with Tommy Cooper* (National Tour), *Ex* (Soho Theatre), *The Schools' Theatre Festival* (Young Vic), *The Real McCoy – Reconnected* (Hackney Empire, Broadway Catford), *My Real War 1914-?* (Trafalgar Studios and National Tour), and *Cooking With Elvis* (Lyceum Theatre, Crewe). His work has been extensively featured in exhibitions, most recently as part of the *Transformation and Revelation: UK Design for Performance* in Cardiff. He is also Director of the Questors Youth Theatre, the largest youth theatre in London.

Elliot Griggs | Lighting Designer

Productions at the Finborough Theatre include *Dream of Perfect Sleep*, *John Ferguson*, *Spokesong* , *Over The Bridge*, *Facts*, *Somersaults*, *The Soft of Her Palm*, *Crush*, *Perchance to Dream*, *Portraits*, *And I and Silence* and *Northern Star*.

Trained at the Royal Academy of Dramatic Art.

Theatre includes *Fleabag* (Soho Theatre and Tour), *CommonWealth* (Almeida Theatre), *The Boy Who Kicked Pigs* (Jackson's Lane Theatre and The Lowry, Manchester), *He Had Hairy Hands* (New Diorama Theatre and National Tour), *Ablutions* (Bike Shed Theatre, Exeter and Tour), *MEAT* (Theatre503), *Belleville Rendez-Vous* (Greenwich Theatre), *Lagan* (Ovalhouse), *Folk Contraption* (Southbank Centre), *Infanticide* (Camden People's Theatre), *Bitter Pleasures for a Sour Generation* (Soho Theatre), *Blues In The Night*, *Joe/Boy* (The Last Refuge), *Love Re:Imagined* (Only Connect Central) *Big Sean, Mikey and Me* (Tristan Bates Theatre), *The Custard Boys* (Tabard Theatre), *Brightest and Best* (Half Moon Theatre), *Dealing With Clair*, *One Minute*, *Nocturnal*, *Dirty Butterfly*, *Our Town* (Royal Academy of Dramatic Art), *The Mercy Seat* (Royal Shakespeare Company at the Capital Centre, Warwick), *The Lady's Not For Burning*, *West Side Story*, *By the Bog of Cats*, *'Tis Pity She's a Whore*, *Elephant's Graveyard* (Warwick Arts Centre), *Much Ado About Nothing* (Belgrade Theatre, Coventry) and *Dido and Aeneas* (St. Paul's Church, London and Tour).

His awards for lighting design include the Francis Reid Award from the Association of Lighting Designers and the ShowLight Award from the National Student Drama Festival.

Max Pappenheim | Sound Designer

Productions at the Finborough Theatre include, as a sound designer, *Variation on a Theme*, *The Hard Man*, *Black Jesus*, *Summer Day's Dream*, *The Hospital at the Time of the Revolution*, *Somersaults*, *The Soft of Her Palm and The Fear of Breathing*; and, as a director, *Perchance to Dream*, *Nothing is the End of the World (Except for The End of the World)* and *Dream of Perfect Sleep*.

Sound Design and Composition includes *Johnny Got His Gun*, *Three Sisters*, *Fiji Land*, *Our Ajax* (Southwark Playhouse), *Mrs Lowry and Son* (Trafalgar Studios), *CommonWealth* (Almeida Theatre), *Being Tommy Cooper* (National Tour), *Irma Vep*, *Borderland*, *Kafka v Kafka* (Brockley Jack Studio Theatre), *Four Corners One Heart* (Theatre503), *Freefall* (New Wimbledon Theatre Studio), *Awkward Conversations with Animals I've F*cked* (Underbelly, Edinburgh) and *Below the Belt* (Edinburgh Festival). As associate sound designer, *The Island* (The Young Vic).

Max was nominated for OffWestEnd Awards for Best Sound Designer in 2012 and 2014.

Anna Lewis | Costume Designer

Productions at the Finborough Theatre include *The White Carnation* which transferred to the Jermyn Street Theatre.

Read English Literature at Somerville College, University of Oxford. Set Designs include *The Sorcerer* (Buxton Opera House) and *Twelfth Night* (International tour to Japan, Bodleian Library Oxford, Southwark Playhouse, Mill Studio Guildford). Costume Designs include *The Nativity Goes Wrong*, *Look Back in Anger* and *Miss Julie* (Reading Rep). Set and Costume Designs include *Bound* (Pegasus Theatre, Oxford), *Middle England* (Burton Taylor Studio, Oxford), *Ghosts* (Greenwich Theatre), *The Hothouse*, *The Picture of Dorian Grey*, *The Seagull*, *A Streetcar Named Desire* (Oxford Playhouse). Assistant Costume Designs include *The Keepers of Infinite Space* (Park Theatre), *The Hotel Plays* (Langham Hotel) and the Dorfman Opening Gala (National Theatre). Assistant Set and Costume Designs include *Ace of Clubs* (Union Theatre). Film includes, as Production Designer, *Round and Round the Garden*, *Mary* and *The Wishing Horse*. As Costume Designer, *The Sanctuary of Collel*, nominated for an award for achievement in costume in the Southampton Film Festival. Anna is also part of the costume team for Secret Cinema and has worked as a costume assistant on eight of their large scale projects including *Dirty Dancing*, *Millers Crossing*, *The Grand Budapest Hotel* and, most recently, *Back to the Future*.

Axa Hynes | Casting Director

Axa is a freelance Casting Director. Axa started her career working as a talent agent at Olivia Bell Management. During her seven years as a talent agent, she completed her degree in Theatre Studies and Psychology, then her Masters with Distinction in Applied Theatre: Drama in Community and Educational Contexts at Goldsmiths University. She has since worked at The Young Vic, Talawa Theatre Company and the Unicorn Theatre. She currently works in the National Theatre Learning Department.

Shannon Martin | Stage Manager

Trained in Stage and Costume Management at the Guildhall School of Music and Drama. Productions at the Guildhall School of Music and Drama include *Grand Hotel*, *Hamlet*, *The Seagull*, *Rags*, *May 08*, *The Laramie Project*, *Twelfth Night*, *Opera Triple Bill*, *Nicholas Nickleby - Part 2* and *Blood Wedding*.

Professional productions include MJ-UK Music and Arts Summer Touring Project (Cirencester and Cornwall), *West End Eurovision* (Dominion Theatre), *Aladdin, Snow White and the Seven Dwarfs* (Royal Spa Centre, Royal Leamington Spa), *Dick Whittington* (Theatre Royal Stratford East), *West Side Story* (New Wimbledon Theatre), *42nd Street* (Albany Theatre, Coventry), *The Big Noise Festival* (The Bussey Building, Peckham Rye), *Muppets: Most Wanted* (Pinewood Studios), *Downton Abbey* (Ealing Studios) and *Sweeney Todd: The Demon Barber of Fleet Street* (Longborough Festival Opera).

Daniel Bailey | Assistant Director

Daniel is currently Resident Assistant Director at The Finborough Theatre. He was previously Resident Director at the National Theatre Studio.

Daniel studied Modern Drama at Brunel University before participating in The Young Vic's Young Directors' programme. Daniel runs the theatre company New Heritage Theatre, which works with new writers and theatre makers to produce thought provoking and challenging work for all audiences. Direction includes *Satanic Panic* (Drayton Arms Theatre), *My Darling Wife* (Talawa Firsts), *Pre Judgement Day* and *Covered* (New Heritage Theatre). Assistant Direction includes *Inherit the Wind* (New Vic Theatre, Stoke), *Lonely Londoners*, *Rules for Living* and *Hotel* (all National Theatre Studio workshop). Short film includes *Malachi* and *Y.O.L.O Therapy*.

Aidan Grounds founded ABG productions in April 2013. He is a recipient of the Stage One Bursary for New Producers and is mentored by Caro Newling. For ABG Productions, theatre includes *Armstrong's War* at the Finborough Theatre and *Jekyll and Hyde* at the Southwark Playhouse. Film includes *The Wishing Horse* with Richard E. Grant (Award of Excellence *Best Shorts Competition*). Aidan is also Executive Director at Reading Repertory Theatre.

Hannah Groombridge has previously worked with ABG on two film projects. Theatre includes *Dido and Aeneas/Young Wife* (King's Head Theatre) and *The Picture of John Gray* (Old Red Lion Theatre). Hannah is the current Resident Producer at the Oxford Playhouse and Magdalen College School. She is also a member of the BBC Production Talent Pool.

ABG Productions Ltd, a company limited by shares. Registered in England and Wales no. 8412125. Registered Office: 2 Castle Court, 176 Castelnau, London, SW13 9DH

Finborough Theatre Commissions
Rachel is a Finborough Theatre commission. Finborough Theatre
commissions are works specially chosen for the Finborough Theatre
by Artistic Director Neil McPherson, and either produced in-house, or in
partnership with some of the UK's most exciting producers.

Production Acknowledgements
The production of *Rachel* at the Finborough Theatre was developed
with the support of the National Theatre Studio, the Stage One Bursary
for New Producers and Arts Council England.

With special thanks to
WorkSpace, Percelle Ascott, Adam Baghdadi, Olivia Bell, Pippa Bennett-
Warner, Sharon D Clarke, Emma Cookson, Alfred Enoch, Paapa
Essiedu, Madge Foster, Masha Gindler, Adrian and Krishna Grounds,
Alexandra Hamburger, Thelma Holt CBE, Colin Ince, Dominic James
Grant, Jenny Killick, Jamie MacDonagh, Simon Manyonda, Caro
Newling, Abigail Pickard Price, Emily Precious, Malcolm Taylor, The
Library of Congress.

FINBOROUGH | THEATRE
VIBRANT **NEW WRITING** | UNIQUE **REDISCOVERIES**

"A disproportionately valuable component of the London theatre ecology. Its programme combines new writing and revivals, in selections intelligent and audacious." *Financial Times*

"The tiny but mighty Finborough… one of the best batting averages of any London company." Ben Brantley, *The New York Times*

"The Finborough Theatre, under the artistic direction of Neil McPherson, has been earning a place on the must-visit list with its eclectic, smartly curated slate of new works and neglected masterpieces." *Vogue*

Founded in 1980, the multi-award-winning Finborough Theatre presents plays and music theatre, concentrated exclusively on vibrant new writing and unique rediscoveries from the 19th and 20th centuries. Behind the scenes, we continue to discover and develop a new generation of theatre makers – through our Literary team, and our programmes for both interns and Resident Assistant Directors.

Despite remaining completely unsubsidised, the Finborough Theatre has an unparalleled track record of attracting the finest creative talent who go on to become leading voices in British theatre. Under Artistic Director Neil McPherson, it has discovered some of the UK's most exciting new playwrights including Laura Wade, James Graham, Mike Bartlett, Sarah Grochala, Jack Thorne, Simon Vinnicombe, Alexandra Wood, Al Smith, Nicholas de Jongh and Anders Lustgarten; and directors including Blanche McIntyre.

Artists working at the theatre in the 1980s included Clive Barker, Rory Bremner, Nica Burns, Kathy Burke, Ken Campbell, Jane Horrocks and Claire Dowie. In the 1990s, the Finborough Theatre first became known for new writing including Naomi Wallace's first play *The War Boys*; Rachel Weisz in David Farr's *Neville Southall's Washbag*; four plays by Anthony Neilson including *Penetrator* and *The Censor*, both of which transferred to the Royal Court Theatre; and new plays by Richard Bean, Lucinda Coxon, David Eldridge, Tony Marchant and Mark Ravenhill. New writing development included the premieres of modern classics such as Mark Ravenhill's *Shopping and F***ing*, Conor McPherson's *This Lime Tree Bower*, Naomi Wallace's *Slaughter City* and Martin McDonagh's *The Pillowman*.

Since 2000, new British plays have included Laura Wade's London debut *Young Emma*, commissioned for the Finborough Theatre; two one-woman shows by Miranda Hart; James Graham's *Albert's Boy* with Victor Spinetti; Sarah Grochala's *S27*; Peter Nichols' *Lingua Franca*, which transferred Off-Broadway; and West End transfers for Joy Wilkinson's *Fair*; Nicholas de Jongh's *Plague Over England*; and Jack Thorne's *Fanny and Faggot*. The late Miriam Karlin made her last stage appearance in *Many Roads to Paradise* in 2008. UK premieres of foreign plays have included Brad Fraser's *Wolfboy*; Lanford Wilson's *Sympathetic Magic*; Larry Kramer's *The Destiny of Me*; Tennessee Williams' *Something Cloudy, Something Clear*; the English premiere of Robert McLellan's Scots language classic, *Jamie the Saxt*; and three West End transfers – Frank McGuinness' *Gates of Gold* with William Gaunt and John Bennett; Joe DiPietro's *F***ing Men*; and Craig Higginson's *Dream of the Dog* with Dame Janet Suzman.

Rediscoveries of neglected work – most commissioned by the Finborough Theatre – have included the first London revivals of Rolf Hochhuth's *Soldiers* and *The Representative*; both parts of Keith Dewhurst's *Lark Rise to Candleford*; *The Women's War*, an evening of original suffragette plays; *Etta Jenks* with Clarke Peters and Daniela Nardini; Noël Coward's first play, *The Rat Trap*; Charles Wood's *Jingo* with Susannah Harker; Emlyn Williams' *Accolade*; Lennox Robinson's *Drama at Inish* with Celia Imrie and Paul O'Grady; John Van Druten's *London Wall* which transferred to St James' Theatre; and J. B. Priestley's *Cornelius* which transferred to a sell out Off Broadway run in New York City.

Music Theatre has included the new (premieres from Grant Olding, Charles Miller, Michael John LaChuisa, Adam Guettel, Andrew Lippa, Paul Scott Goodman, and Adam Gwon's *Ordinary Days* which transferred to the West End) and the old (the UK premiere of Rodgers and Hammerstein's *State Fair* which also transferred to the West End), and the acclaimed 'Celebrating British Music Theatre' series, reviving forgotten British musicals.

The Finborough Theatre won *The Stage* Fringe Theatre of the Year Award in 2011, *London Theatre Reviews'* Empty Space Peter Brook Award in 2010 and 2012, the Empty Space Peter Brook Award's Dan Crawford Pub Theatre Award in 2005 and 2008, the Empty Space Peter Brook Mark Marvin Award in 2004, and swept the board with eight awards at the 2012 OffWestEnd Awards including Best Artistic Director and Best Director for the second year running. *Accolade* was named Best Fringe Show of 2011 by *Time Out*. It is the only unsubsidised theatre ever to be awarded the Pearson Playwriting Award (now the Channel 4 Playwrights Scheme) nine times. Three bursary holders (Laura Wade, James Graham and Anders Lustgarten) have also won the Catherine Johnson Award for Pearson Best Play.

www.finboroughtheatre.co.uk

FINBOROUGH | THEATRE
VIBRANT **NEW WRITING** | UNIQUE **REDISCOVERIES**

118 Finborough Road, London SW10 9ED
admin@finboroughtheatre.co.uk
www.finboroughtheatre.co.uk

The Finborough Theatre has the support of the Channel 4 Playwrights' Scheme, sponsored by Channel 4 Television and supported by The Peggy Ramsay Foundation.

Supported by DLA PIPER

The Richard Carne Trust richardcarnetrust.org

The Finborough Theatre is a member of the Independent Theatre Council, the Society of Independent Theatres, Musical Theatre Network, The Friends of Brompton Cemetery and The Earl's Court Society www.earlscourtsociety.org.uk

Mailing
Email admin@finboroughtheatre.co.uk or give your details to our Box Office staff to join our free email list. If you would like to be sent a free season leaflet every three months, just include your postal address and postcode.

 Follow Us Online
www.facebook.com/FinboroughTheatre
www.twitter.com/finborough

Feedback
We welcome your comments, complaints and suggestions. Write to Finborough Theatre, 118 Finborough Road, London SW10 9ED or email us at admin@finboroughtheatre.co.uk

Playscripts
Many of the Finborough Theatre's plays have been published and are on sale from our website.

Finborough Theatre T Shirts
Finborough Theatre T Shirts are now on sale from the Box Office, available in Small and Medium £7.00.

Friends

The Finborough Theatre is a registered charity. We receive no public funding, and rely solely on the support of our audiences. Please do consider supporting us by becoming a member of our Friends of the Finborough Theatre scheme. There are various categories of Friends, each offering a wide range of benefits.

Richard Tauber Friends – Val Bond. James Brown. Tom Erhardt. Bill Hornby. Richard Jackson. Mike Lewendon. John Lawson. Harry MacAuslan. Mark and Susan Nichols. Sarah Thomas. Kathryn McDowall. Barry Serjent.

Lionel Monckton Friends – S. Harper. Philip G Hooker. Martin and Wendy Kramer. Deborah Milner. Maxine and Eric Reynolds.

William Terriss Friends – Stuart Ffoulkes. Leo and Janet Liebster. Peter Lobl. Paul and Lindsay Kennedy. Corinne Rooney. Jon and NoraLee Sedmak.

Smoking is not permitted in the auditorium and the use of cameras and recording equipment is strictly prohibited.

In accordance with the requirements of the Royal Borough of Kensington and Chelsea:

1. The public may leave at the end of the performance by all doors and such doors must at that time be kept open.

2. All gangways, corridors, staircases and external passageways intended for exit shall be left entirely free from obstruction whether permanent or temporary.

3. Persons shall not be permitted to stand or sit in any of the gangways intercepting the seating or to sit in any of the other gangways.

The Finborough Theatre is licensed by the Royal Borough of Kensington and Chelsea to The Steam Industry, a registered charity and a company limited by guarantee. Registered in England and Wales no. 3448268. Registered Charity no. 1071304. Registered Office: 118 Finborough Road, London SW10 9ED.

The Steam Industry is under the overall Artistic Direction of Phil Willmott. www.philwillmott.co.uk

RACHEL

Angelina Weld Grimké

RACHEL

OBERON BOOKS
LONDON

WWW.OBERONBOOKS.COM

Originally published in 1920 by The Cornhill Company, Boston.

This facsimile edition of the Cornhill text published in 2014
by Oberon Books Ltd
521 Caledonian Road, London N7 9RH
Tel: +44 (0) 20 7607 3637 / Fax: +44 (0) 20 7607 3629
e-mail: info@oberonbooks.com
www.oberonbooks.com

A catalogue record for this book is available from the British
Library.

PB ISBN: 978-1-78319-187-1
E ISBN: 978-1-78319-686-9

Visit www.oberonbooks.com to read more about all our books
and to buy them. You will also find features, author interviews and
news of any author events, and you can sign up for e-newsletters
so that you're always first to hear about our new releases.

CHARACTERS

Mrs Mary Loving, *a widow.*
Rachel Loving, *her daughter.*
Thomas Loving, *her son.*
Jimmy Mason, *a small boy.*
John Strong, *a friend of the family.*
Mrs. Lane, *a caller.*
Ethel Lane, *her daughter.*
Mary,
Nancy,
Edith,
Jenny,
Louise,
Martha,
      little friends of Rachel.

Time: The first decade of the Twentieth Century.

    Act I.   October 16th.
    Act II. October 16th, four years later.
    Act III. One week later.

Place: A northern city. The living room in the small apartment of Mrs. Loving.

      All of the characters are colored.

ACT I

RACHEL

ACT I.

*The scene is a room scrupulously neat and clean and plainly
furnished. The walls are painted green, the woodwork,
white. In the rear at the left an open doorway leads
into a hall. Its bare, green wall and white baseboard
are all that can be seen of it. It leads into the other
rooms of the flat. In the centre of the rear wall of
the room is a window. It is shut. The white sash
curtains are pushed to right and left as far as they will
go. The green shade is rolled up to the top. Through
the window can be seen the red bricks of a house wall,
and the tops of a couple of trees moving now and then
in the wind. Within the window, and just below the
sill, is a shelf upon which are a few potted plants.
Between the window and the door is a bookcase full of
books and above it, hanging on the wall, a simply
framed, inexpensive copy of Millet's "The Reapers."
There is a run extending from the right center to just
below the right upper entrance. It is the vestibule of
the flat. Its open doorway faces the left wall. In the
right wall near the front is another window. Here the
sash curtains are drawn together and the green shade
is partly lowered. The window is up from the bottom.
Through it street noises can be heard. In front of this
window is an open, threaded sewing-machine. Some
frail, white fabric is lying upon it. There is a chair in*

3

front of the machine and at the machine's left a small table covered with a green cloth. In the rear of the left wall and directly opposite to the entrance to the flat is the doorway leading into the kitchenette, dishes on shelves can be seen behind glass doors.

In the center of the left wall is a fireplace with a grate in it for coals; over this is a wooden mantel painted white. In the center is a small clock. A pair of vases, green and white in coloring, one at each end, complete the ornaments. Over the mantel is a narrow mirror; and over this, hanging on the wall, Burne-Jones' "Golden Stairs," simply framed. Against the front end of the left wall is an upright piano with a stool in front of it. On top is music neatly piled. Hanging over the piano is Raphael's "Sistine Madonna." In the center of the floor is a green rug, and in the center of this, a rectangular dining-room table, the long side facing front. It is covered with a green table-cloth. Three dining-room chairs are at the table, one at either end and one at the rear facing front. Above the table is a chandelier with four gas jets enclosed by glass globes. At the right front center is a rather shabby arm-chair upholstered in green.

Left and right from the spectator's point of view.

Before the sewing-machine, Mrs. Loving is seated. She looks worried. She is sewing swiftly and deftly by hand upon a waist in her lap. It is a white, beautiful thing and she sews upon it delicately. It is about half-past four in the afternoon; and the light is failing. Mrs. Loving pauses in her sewing, rises and lets the window-shade near her go up to the top. She pushes the sash-curtains to either side, the corner of a red brick house wall being thus brought into view. She shivers slightly, then pushes the window down at the bottom and lowers it a trifle from the top. The street noises become less distinct. She takes off her thimble, rubs her hands gently, puts the thimble on again, and looks at the clock on the mantel. She then reseats herself, with her chair as close to the window as possible and begins to sew. Presently a key is heard, and the door opens and shuts noisily. Rachel comes in from the vestibule. In her left arm she carries four or five books strapped together; under her right, a roll of music. Her hat is twisted over her left ear and her hair is falling in tendrils about her face. She brings into the room with her the spirit of abounding life, health, joy, youth. Mrs. Loving pauses, needle in hand, as soon as she hears the turning key and the banging door. There is a smile on her face. For a second, mother and daughter smile at each other. Then Rachel throws her books upon the dining-room table, places the music there also, but with care, and rushing to her mother, gives her a bear hug and a kiss.

RACHEL: Ma dear! dear, old Ma dear!

MRS. LOVING: Look out for the needle, Rachel! The waist! Oh, Rachel!

RACHEL (*On her knees and shaking her finger directly under her mother's nose.*) : You old, old fraud! You know you adore being hugged. I've a good mind . . .

MRS. LOVING: Now, Rachel, please! Besides, I know your tricks. You think you can make me forget you are late. What time is it?

RACHEL (*Looking at the clock and expressing surprise*) : Jiminy Xmas! (*Whistles*) Why, it's five o'clock!

MRS. LOVING (*Severely*) : Well!

RACHEL (*Plaintively*) : Now, Ma dear, you're going to be horrid and cross.

MRS. LOVING (*Laughing*): Really, Rachel, that expression is not particularly affecting, when your hat is over your ear, and you look, with your hair over your eyes, exactly like some one's pet poodle. I wonder if you are ever going to grow up and be ladylike.

RACHEL: Oh! Ma dear, I hope not, not for the longest time, two long, long years at least. I just want to be silly and irresponsible, and have you to love and torment, and, of course, Tom, too.

MRS. LOVING (*Smiling down at Rachel*): You'll not make me forget, young lady. Why are you late, Rachel?

RACHEL: Well, Ma dear, I'm your pet poodle, and my hat is over my ear, and I'm late, for the loveliest reason.

MRS. LOVING: Don't be silly, Rachel.

RACHEL: That may sound silly, but it isn't. And please don't "Rachel" me so much. It was honestly one whole hour ago when I opened the front door down stairs. I know it was, because I heard the postman telling some one it was four o'clock. Well, I climbed the first flight, and was just starting up the second, when a little shrill voice said, "'Lo!" I raised my eyes, and there, half-way up the stairs, sitting in the middle of a step, was just the dearest, cutest, darlingest little brown baby boy you ever saw. "'Lo! yourself," I said. "What are you doing, and who are you anyway?" "I'm Jimmy; and I'm widing to New York on the choo-choo tars." As he looked entirely too young to be going such a distance by himself, I asked him if I might go too. For a minute or two he considered the question and me very seriously, and then he said, "'Es," and made room for me on the step beside him. We've been everywhere: New York, Chicago, Boston, London, Paris and Oshkosh. I wish you could have heard him say that last place. I suggested going there just to hear him. Now, Ma dear, is it any wonder I am late? See all the places we have been in just one "teeny, weeny" hour? We would have been traveling yet, but his horrid, little mother came out and called him in. They're in the flat below, the new people. But before he went, Ma dear, he said the "cunningest" thing. He said, "Will you tum out an' p'ay wif me aden in two minutes?" I nearly hugged him to death, and it's a wonder my hat is on my head at all. Hats are such unimportant nuisances anyway!

MRS. LOVING: Unimportant nuisances! What ridiculous language you do use, Rachel! Well, I'm no prophet, but I see very distinctly what is going to happen. This little brown baby will be living here night and day. You're not happy unless some child is trailing along in your rear.

RACHEL (*Mischievously*): Now, Ma dear, whose a hypocrite? What? I suppose you don't like children! I can tell you one thing, though, it won't be my fault if he isn't here night and day. Oh, I wish he were all mine, every bit of him! Ma dear, do you suppose that "she woman" he calls mother would let him come up here until it is time for him to go to bed? I'm going down there this minute. (*Rises impetuously*).

MRS. LOVING: Rachel, for Heaven's sake! No! I am entirely too busy and tired today without being bothered with a child romping around in here.

RACHEL (*Reluctantly and a trifle petulantly*): Very well, then. (*For several moments she watches her mother, who has begun to sew again. The displeasure vanishes from her face*). Ma dear!

MRS. LOVING: Well.

RACHEL: Is there anything wrong today?

MRS. LOVING: I'm just tired, chickabiddy, that's all.

RACHEL (*Moves over to the table. Mechanically takes off her hat and coat and carries them out into the entryway* of the flat. *She returns and goes to the looking glass over the fireplace and tucks in the tendrils of her hair in rather a preoccupied manner. The electric doorbell rings. She returns to the speaking tube in the vestibule. Her voice is heard answering*): Yes!—Yes!—No, I'm not Mrs. Loving. She's here, yes!—What? Oh! come right up! (*Appearing in the doorway*). Ma dear, it's some man, who is coming for Mrs. Strong's waist.

MRS. LOVING (*Pausing and looking at Rachel*): It is probably her son. She said she would send for it this afternoon. (*Rachel disappears. A door is heard opening and closing. There is the sound of a man's voice. Rachel ushers in Mr. John Strong.*)

STRONG (*Bowing pleasantly to Mrs. Loving*): Mrs. Loving? (*Mrs. Loving bows, puts down her sewing, rises and goes toward Strong*). My name is Strong. My mother asked me to come by and get her waist this afternoon. She hoped it would be finished.

MRS. LOVING: Yes, Mr. Strong, it is all ready. If you'll sit down a minute, I'll wrap it up for you. (*She goes into hallway leading to other rooms in flat*).

RACHEL (*Manifestly ill at ease at being left alone with a stranger; attempting, however, to be the polite hostess*): Do sit down, Mr. Strong. (*They both sit*).

RACHEL (*Nervously after a pause*): It's a very pleasant day, isn't it, Mr. Strong?
STRONG: Yes, very. (*He leans back composedly, his hat on his knee, the faintest expression of amusement in his eyes*).

RACHEL (*After a pause*): It's quite a climb up to our flat, don't you think?
STRONG: Why, no! It didn't strike me so. I'm not old enough yet to mind stairs.

RACHEL: (*Nervously*) : Oh! I didn't mean that you are old! Anyone can see you are quite young, that is, of course, not too young, but,—(*Strong laughs quietly*). There! I don't blame you for laughing. I'm always clumsy just like that.

MRS. LOVING (*Calling from the other room*) : Rachel, bring me a needle and the sixty cotton, please.

RACHEL: All right, Ma dear! (*Rummages for the cotton in the machine drawer, and upsets several spools upon the floor. To Strong*): You see! I can't even get a spool of cotton without spilling things all over the floor. (*Strong smiles, Rachel picks up the spools and finally gets the cotton and needle*). Excuse me! (*Goes out door leading to other rooms. Strong left to himself, looks around casually. The "Golden Stairs" interests him and the "Sistine Madonna."*)

RACHEL (*Reenters, evidently continuing her function of hostess*): We were talking about the climb to our flat, weren't we? You see, when you're poor, you have to live in a top flat. There is always a compensation, though; we have bully—I mean nice air, better light, a lovely view, and nobody "thud-thudding" up and down over our heads night and day. The people below have our "thud-thudding," and it must be something *awful,* especially when Tom and I play "Ivanhoe" and have a tournament up here. We're entirely too old, but we still play. Ma dear rather dreads the climb up three flights, so Tom and I do all the errands. We don't mind climbing the stairs, particularly when we go up two or three at a time,—that is—Tom still does. I can't, Ma dear stopped me. (*Sighs*). I've got to grow up it seems.

STRONG (*Evidently amused*): It is rather hard being a girl, isn't it?

RACHEL: Oh, no! It's not hard at all. That's the trouble; they won't let me be a girl. I'd love to be.

MRS. LOVING (*Reentering with parcel. She smiles*): My chatterbox, I see, is entertaining you, Mr. Strong. I'm sorry to have kept you waiting, but I forgot, I found, to sew the ruching in the neck. I hope everything is satisfactory. If it isn't, I'll be glad to make any changes.

STRONG (*Who has risen upon her entrance*): Thank you, Mrs. Loving, I'm sure everything is all right. (*He takes the package and bows to her and Rachel. He moves towards the vestibule, Mrs. Loving following him. She passes through the doorway first. Before leaving, Strong turns for a second and looks back quietly at Rachel. He goes out too. Rachel returns to the mirror, looks at her face for a second, and then begins to touch and pat her hair lightly and delicately here and there. Mrs. Loving returns*).

RACHEL (*Still at the glass*): He *was* rather nice, wasn't he, Ma dear?—for a man? (*Laughs*). I guess my reason's a vain one,—he let me do all the talking. (*Pauses*). Strong? Strong? Ma dear, is his mother the little woman with the sad, black eyes?

MRS. LOVING (*Resuming her sewing; sitting before the machine*). Yes. I was rather curious, I confess, to see this son of hers. The whole time I'm fitting her she talks of nothing else. She worships him. (*Pauses*). It's rather a sad case, I believe. She is a widow. Her husband was a doctor and left her a little money. She came up from the South to educate this boy. Both of them worked hard and the boy got through college. Three months he hunted for work that a college man might expect to get. You see he had the tremendous handicap of being colored. As the two of them had to live, one day, without her knowing it, he hired himself out as a waiter. He has been

10

one now for two years. He is evidently goodness itself to his mother.

RACHEL (*Slowly and thoughtfully*) : Just because he is *colored!* (*Pauses*). We sing a song at school, I believe, about "The land of the free and the home of the brave." What an amusing nation it is.

MRS. LOVING (*Watching Rachel anxiously*) : Come, Rachel, you haven't time for "amusing nations." Remember, you haven't practised any this afternoon. And put your books away ; don't leave them on the table. You didn't practise any this morning either, did you?

RACHEL : No, Ma dear,—didn't wake up in time. (*Goes to the table and in an abstracted manner puts books on the bookcase; returns to the table; picks up the roll of sheet music she has brought home with her; brightens; impulsively*) Ma dear, just listen to this lullaby. It's the sweetest thing. I was so "daffy" over it, one of the girls at school lent it to me. (*She rushes to the piano with the music and plays the accompaniment through softly and then sings, still softly and with great expression, Jessie Gaynor's "Slumber Boat"*)—

> Baby's boat's the silver moon ;
> Sailing in the sky,
> Sailing o'er the sea of sleep,
> While the clouds float by.

> Sail, baby, sail,
> Out upon that sea,
> Only don't forget to sail
> Back again to me.

Baby's fishing for a dream,
    Fishing near and far,
His line a silver moonbeam is,
    His bait a silver star.

Sail, baby, sail, etc.

Listen, Ma dear, right here. Isn't it lovely? (*Plays and sings very softly and slowly*):
    "Only don't forget to sail
      Back again to me."
(*Pauses; in hushed tones*) Ma dear, it's so beautiful—it—it hurts.

MRS. LOVING (*Quietly*): Yes, dear, it is pretty.

RACHEL (*For several minutes watches her mother's profile from the piano stool. Her expression is rather wistful*): Ma dear!

MRS. LOVING: Yes, Rachel.

RACHEL: What's the matter?

MRS. LOVING (*Without turning*): Matter! What do you mean?

RACHEL: I don't know. I just *feel* something is not quite right with you.

MRS. LOVING: I'm only tired—that's all.

RACHEL: Perhaps. But—(*Watches her mother a moment or two longer; shakes her head; turns back to the piano. She is thoughtful; looks at her hands in her lap*). Ma dear, wouldn't it be nice if we could keep all the babies in the world—always little babies? Then they'd be always little, and cunning, and lovable; and they could never grow up, then, and—and—be bad. I'm so sorry for mothers, whose little babies—grow up—and—and—are bad.

MRS. LOVING (*Startled; controlling herself, looks at Rachel anxiously, perplexedly. Rachel's eyes are still on her hands. Attempting a light tone*): Come, Rachel, what experience have you had with mothers whose babies have grown up to be bad? You—you talk like an old, old woman.

RACHEL (*Without raising her eyes, quietly*): I *know* I'm not old; but, just the same I know that is true. (*Softly*) And I'm so sorry for the mothers.

MRS. LOVING (*With a forced laugh*): Well, Miss Methuselah, how do you happen to know all this? Mothers whose babies grow up to be bad don't, as a rule, parade their faults before the world.

RACHEL: That's just it—that's *how* you know. They don't talk at all.

MRS. LOVING (*Involuntarily*): Oh! (*Ceases to sew; looks at Rachel sharply; she is plainly worried. There is a long silence. Presently Rachel raises her eyes to Raphael's "Madonna" over the piano. Her expression becomes rapt; then, very softly, her eyes still on the picture, she plays and sings Nevin's "Mighty Lak A Rose"*)—

> Sweetest li'l feller,
>   Ev'rybody knows;
> Dunno what to call him,
>   But he mighty lak' a rose!
> Lookin' at his Mammy
>   Wid eyes so shiny blue,
> Mek' you think that heav'n
>   Is comin' clost ter you!
>
> W'en his dar a sleepin'
>   In his li'l place
> Think I see de angels
>   Lookin' thro' de lace.
> W'en de dark is fallin',

W'en de shadders creep,
Den dey comes on tip-toe,
Ter kiss him in his sleep.

Sweetest li'l feller, etc.

(*With head still raised, after she has finished, she closes
her eyes.   Half to herself and slowly*) I think the loveliest
thing of all the lovely things in this world is just (*almost
in a whisper*) being a mother!

MRS. LOVING (*Turns and laughs*) : Well, of all the startling
children, Rachel! I am getting to feel, when you're
around as though I'm shut up with dynamite.   What
next?   (*Rachel rises, goes slowly to her mother, and
kneels down beside her.   She does not touch her mother*).
Why so serious, chickabiddy?

RACHEL (*Slowly and quietly*) : It is not kind to laugh at
sacred things.   When you laughed, it was as though you
laughed—at God!

MRS. LOVING (*Startled*) : Rachel!

RACHEL (*Still quietly*) : It's true.   It was the best in me
that said that—it was God!   (*Pauses*).   And, Ma dear,
if I believed that I should grow up and not be a mother,
I'd pray to die now.   I've thought about it a lot, Ma dear,
and once I dreamed, and a voice said to me—oh! it was so
real—"Rachel, you are to be a mother to little children."
Wasn't that beautiful?   Ever since I have known how
Mary felt at the "Annunciation."   (*Almost in a whisper*)
God spoke to me through some one, and I believe.   And
it has explained so much to me.   I know now why I just
can't resist any child.   I have to love it—it calls me—it—
draws me.   I want to take care of it, wash it, dress it, live
for it.   I want the feel of its little warm body against
me, its breath on my neck, its hands against my face.

14

(*Pauses thoughtfully for a few moments*). Ma dear, here's something I don't understand: I love the little black and brown babies best of all. There is something about them that—that—clutches at my heart. Why—why—should they be—oh!—pathetic? I don't understand. It's dim. More than the other babies, I feel that I must protect them. They're in danger, but from what? I don't know. I've tried so hard to understand, but I can't. (*Her face radiant and beautiful*). Ma dear, I think their white teeth and the clear whites of their big black eyes and their dimples everywhere—are—are (*Breaks off*). And, Ma dear, because I love them best, I pray God every night to give me, when I grow up, little black and brown babies—to protect and guard. (*Wistfully*). Now, Ma dear, don't you see why you must never laugh at me again? Dear, dear, Ma dear? (*Buries her head in her mother's lap and sobs*).

MRS. LOVING (*For a few seconds, sits as though dazed, and then instinctively begins to caress the head in her lap. To herself*) And I suppose my experience is every mother's. Sooner or later—of a sudden she finds her own child a stranger to her. (*To Rachel, very tenderly*) Poor little girl! Poor little chickabiddy!

RACHEL (*Raising her head*): Why do you say, "Poor little girl," like that? I don't understand. Why, Ma dear, I never saw tears in your eyes before. Is it—is it—because you know the things I do not understand? Oh! it *is* that.

MRS. LOVING (*Simply*): Yes, Rachel, and I cannot save you.

RACHEL: Ma dear, you frighten me. Save me from *what?*

MRS. LOVING: Just life, my little chickabiddy!

RACHEL: Is life so terrible? I had found it mostly beautiful. How can life be terrible, when the world is full of little children?

MRS. LOVING (*Very sadly*): Oh, Rachel! Rachel!

RACHEL: Ma dear, what have I said?

MRS. LOVING (*Forcing a smile*): Why, the truth, of course, Rachel. Life is not terrible when there are little children —and you—and Tom—and a roof over our heads—and work—and food—and clothes—and sleep at night. (*Pauses*). Rachel, I am not myself today. I'm tired. Forget what I've said. Come, chickabiddy, wipe your eyes and smile. That's only an imitation smile, but it's better than none. Jump up now, and light the lamp for me, will you? Tom's late, isn't he? I shall want you to go, too, for the rolls and pie for supper.

RACHEL (*Rises rather wearily and goes into the kitchenette. While she is out of the room Mrs. Loving does not move. She sits staring in front of her. The room for some time has been growing dark. Mrs. Loving can just be seen when Rachel reenters with the lamp. She places it on the small table near her mother, adjusts it, so the light falls on her mother's work, and then lowers the window shades at the windows. She still droops. Mrs. Loving, while Rachel is in the room, is industrious. Rachel puts on her hat and coat listlessly. She does not look in the glass*). Where is the money, Ma dear? I'm ready.

MRS. LOVING: Before you go, Rachel, just give a look at the meat and see if it is cooking all right, will you, dearie?

RACHEL (*Goes out into the kitchenette and presently returns*): It's all right, Ma dear.

MRS. LOVING (*While Rachel is out of the room, she takes her pocket-book out of the machine-drawer, opens it, takes out money and gives it to Rachel upon her return*): A dozen brown rolls, Rachel. Be sure they're brown! And, I guess,—an apple pie. As you and Tom never seem to get enough apple pie, get the largest she has. And here is a quarter. Get some candy—any kind *you* like, Chickabiddy. Let's have a party tonight, I feel extravagant. Why, Rachel! why are you crying?

RACHEL: Nothing, dear Ma dear. I'll be all right when I get in the air. Goodbye! (*Rushes out of the flat. Mrs. Loving sits idle. Presently the outer door of the flat opens and shuts with a bang, and Tom appears. Mrs. Loving begins to work as soon as she hears the banging door*).

TOM: 'Lo, Ma! Where's Sis,—out? The door's off the latch. (*Kisses his mother and hangs hat in entryway*).

MRS. LOVING (*Greeting him with the same beautiful smile with which she greeted Rachel*): Rachel just went after the rolls and pie. She'll be back in a few minutes. You're late, Tommy.

TOM: No, Ma—you forget—it's pay day. (*With decided shyness and awkwardness he hands her his wages*). Here, Ma!

MRS. LOVING (*Proudly counting it*): But, Tommy, this is every bit of it. You'll need some.

TOM: Not yet! (*Constrainedly*) I only wish—. Say, Ma, I hate to see you work so hard. (*Fiercely*) Some day— some day—. (*Breaks off*).

MRS. LOVING: Son, I'm as proud as though you had given me a million dollars.

TOM (*Emphatically*): I may some day,—you see. (*Abruptly changing the subject*): Gee! Ma, I'm hungry. What's for dinner? Smell's good.

MRS. LOVING: Lamb and dumplings and rice.

TOM: Gee! I'm glad I'm living—and a pie too?

MRS. LOVING: Apple pie, Tommy.

TOM: Say, Ma, don't wake me up. And shall "muzzer's" own little boy set the table?

MRS. LOVING: Thank you, Son.

Tom (*Folds the green cloth, hangs it over the back of the arm-chair, gets white table-cloth from kitchenette and sets the table. The whole time he is whistling blithely a popular air. He lights one of the gas jets over the table*): Ma!

Mrs. Loving: Yes, Son.

Tom: I made "squad" today,—I'm quarterback. Five other fellows tried to make it. We'll all have to buy new hats, now.

Mrs. Loving (*With surprise*): Buy new hats! Why?

Tom (*Makes a ridiculous gesture to show that his head and hers are both swelling*): Honest, Ma, I had to carry my hat in my hand tonight,—couldn't even get it to perch aloft.

Mrs. Loving (*Smiling*): Well, I for one, Son, am not going to say anything to make you more conceited.

Tom: You don't *have* to say anything. Why, Ma, ever since I told you, you can almost look down your own back your head is so high. What? (*Mrs. Loving laughs. The outer door of the flat opens and shuts. Rachel's voice is heard*).

Rachel (*Without*): My! that was a "drefful" climb, wasn't it? Ma, I've got something here for you. (*Appears in the doorway carrying packages and leading a little boy by the hand. The little fellow is shy but smiling*). Hello, Tommy! Here, take these things for me. This is Jimmy. Isn't he a dear? Come, Jimmy. (*Tom carries the packages into the kitchenette. Rachel leads Jimmy to Mrs. Loving*). Ma dear, this is my brown baby. I'm going to take him right down stairs again. His mother is as sweet as can be, and let me bring him up just to see you. Jimmy, this is Ma dear. (*Mrs. Loving turns expectantly to see the child. Standing before her, he raises his face to hers with an engaging smile. Suddenly, without word or warning, her body stiffens; her hands grip her sewing convulsively; her eyes stare. She makes no sound).*

RACHEL *(Frightened)*: Ma dear! What is the matter? Tom! Quick! *(Tom reenters and goes to them).*

MRS. LOVING *(Controlling herself with an effort and breathing hard)*: Nothing, dears, nothing. I must be—I am— nervous tonight. *(With a forced smile)* How do-you-do, Jimmy? Now, Rachel—perhaps—don't you think— you had better take him back to his mother? Good-night, Jimmy! *(Eyes the child in a fascinated way the whole time he is in the room. Rachel, very much perturbed, takes the child out).* Tom, open that window, please! There! That's better! *(Still breathing deeply).* What a fool I am!

TOM *(Patting his mother awkwardly on the back)*: You're all pegged out, that's the trouble—working entirely too hard. Can't you stop for the night and go to bed right after supper?

MRS. LOVING: I'll see, Tommy dear. Now, I must look after the supper.

TOM: Huh! Well, I guess not. How old do you think Rachel and I are anyway? I see; you think we'll break some of this be-au-tiful Hav-i-land china, we bought at the "Five and Ten Cent Store." *(To Rachel who has just reentered wearing a puzzled and worried expression. She is without hat and coat).* Say, Rachel, do you think you're old enough?

RACHEL: Old enough for what, Tommy?

TOM: To dish up the supper for Ma.

RACHEL *(With attempted sprightliness)*: Ma dear thinks nothing can go on in this little flat unless she does it. Let's show her a thing or two. *(They bring in the dinner. Mrs. Loving with trembling hands tries to sew. Tom and Rachel watch her covertly. Presently she gets up.)*

Mrs. Loving: I'll be back in a minute, children. (*Goes out the door that leads to the other rooms of the flat. Tom and Rachel look at each other*).

Rachel (*In a low voice keeping her eyes on the door*): Why do you suppose she acted so strangely about Jimmy?

Tom: Don't know—nervous, I guess,—worn out. I wish— (*Breaks off*).

Rachel (*Slowly*): It may be that; but she hasn't been herself this afternoon. I wonder—. Look out! Here she comes!

Tom (*In a whisper*): Liven her up. (*Rachel nods. Mrs. Loving reenters. Both rush to her and lead her to her place at the right end of the table. She smiles and tries to appear cheerful. They sit down, Tom opposite Mrs. Loving and Rachel at the side facing front. Mrs Loving asks grace. Her voice trembles. She helps the children bountifully, herself sparingly. Every once in a while she stops eating and stares blankly into her plate; then, remembering where she is suddenly, looks around with a start and goes on eating. Tom and Rachel appear not to notice her*).

Tom: Ma's "some" cook, isn't she?

Rachel: Is she! Delmonico's isn't in it.

Tom (*Presently*): Say, Rachel, do you remember that Reynolds boy in the fourth year?

Rachel: Yes. You mean the one who is flat-nosed, freckled, and who squints and sneers?

Tom (*Looking at Rachel admiringly*): The same.

Rachel (*Vehemently*): I hate him!

Mrs. Loving: Rachel, you do use such violent language. Why hate him?

Rachel: I do—that's all.

Tom: Ma, if you saw him just once, you'd understand. No one likes him. But, then, what can you expect? His father's in "quod" doing time for something, I don't know just what. One of the fellows says he has a real decent mother, though. She never mentions him in any way, shape or form, he says. Hard on her, isn't it? Bet I'd keep my head shut too;—you'd never get a yap out of me. (*Rachel looks up quickly at her mother; Mrs. Loving stiffens perceptibly, but keeps her eyes on her plate. Rachel catches Tom's eye; silently draws his attention to their mother; and shakes her head warningly at him*).

TOM (*Continuing hastily and clumsily*): Well, anyway, he called me "Nigger" today. If his face isn't black, his eye is.

RACHEL: Good! Oh! Why did you let the other one go?

TOM (*Grinning*): I knew he said things behind my back; but today he was hopping mad, because I made quarterback. He didn't!

RACHEL: Oh, Tommy! How lovely! Ma dear, did you hear that? (*Chants*) Our Tommy's on the team! Our Tommy's on the team!

TOM (*Trying not to appear pleased*): Ma dear, what did I say about er—er "capital" enlargements?

MRS. LOVING (*Smiling*): You're right, Son.

TOM: I hope you got that "capital," Rachel. How's that for Latin knowledge? Eh?

RACHEL: I don't think much of your knowledge, Tommy dear; but (*continuing to chant*) Our Tommy's on the team! Our Tommy's on the team! Our— (*Breaks off*). I've a good mind to kiss you.

TOM (*Threateningly*): Don't you dare.

RACHEL (*Rising and going toward him*): I will! I will! I will!

TOM (*Rising, too, and dodging her*): No, you don't, young lady. (*A tremendous tussle and scuffle ensues*).

Mrs. Loving (*Laughing*): For Heaven's sake! children, do stop playing and eat your supper. (*They nod brightly at each other behind her back and return smiling to the table*).

Rachel (*Sticking out her tongue at Tom*): I will!

Tom (*Mimicking her*): You won't!

Mrs. Loving: Children! (*They eat for a time in silence*).

Rachel: Ma dear, have you noticed Mary Shaw doesn't come here much these days?

Mrs. Loving: Why, that's so, she doesn't. Have you two quarreled?

Rachel: No, Ma dear. (*Uncomfortably*). I—think I know the reason—but I don't like to say, unless I'm certain.

Tom: Well, I know. I've seen her lately with those two girls who have just come from the South. Twice she bowed stiffly, and the last time made believe she didn't see me.

Rachel: Then you think—? Oh! I was afraid it was that.

Tom (*Bitterly*): Yes—we're "niggers"—that's why.

Mrs. Loving (*Slowly and sadly*): Rachel, that's one of the things I can't save you from. I worried considerably about Mary, at first—you do take your friendships so seriously. I knew exactly how it would end. (*Pauses*). And then I saw that if Mary Shaw didn't teach you the lesson—some one else would. They don't want you, dearies, when you and they grow up. You may have everything in your favor—but they don't *dare* to like you.

Rachel: I know all that is generally true—but I had hoped that Mary— (*Breaks off*).

Tom: Well, I guess we can still go on living even if people don't speak to us. I'll never bow to *her* again—that's certain.

MRS. LOVING: But, Son, that wouldn't be polite, if she bowed to you first.

TOM: Can't help it. I guess I can be blind, too.

MRS. LOVING (*Wearily*): Well—perhaps you are right—I don't know. It's the way I feel about it too—but—but I wish my son always to be a *gentleman*.

TOM: If being a *gentleman* means not being a *man*—I don't wish to be one.

RACHEL: Oh! well, perhaps we're wrong about Mary—I hope we are. (*Sighs*). Anyway, let's forget it. Tommy guess what I've got. (*Rises, goes out into entryway swiftly, and returns holding up a small bag*). Ma dear treated. Guess!

TOM: Ma, you're a thoroughbred. Well, let's see—it's—a dozen dill pickles?

RACHEL: Oh! stop fooling.

TOM: I'm not. Tripe?

RACHEL: Silly!

TOM: Hog's jowl?

RACHEL: Ugh! Give it up—quarter-back.

TOM: Pig's feet?

RACHEL (*In pretended disgust*): Oh! Ma dear—send him from the table. It's CANDY!

TOM: Candy? Funny, I never thought of that! And I was just about to say some nice, delicious chitlings. Candy! Well! Well! (*Rachel disdainfully carries the candy to her mother, returns to her own seat with the bag and helps herself. She ignores Tom*).

TOM (*In an aggrieved voice*): You see, Ma, how she treats me. (*In affected tones*) I have a good mind, young lady to punish you, er—er corporeally speaking. Tut! Tut! I have a mind to master thee—I mean—you. Methinks that if I should advance upon you, apply, perchance, two or three digits to your glossy locks and extract—aha!—

say, a strand—you would no more defy me. (*He starts to rise*).

MRS. LOVING (*Quickly and sharply*): Rachel! give Tom the candy and stop playing. (*Rachel obeys. They eat in silence. The old depression returns. When the candy is all gone, Rachel pushes her chair back, and is just about to rise, when her mother, who is very evidently nerving herself for something, stops her*). Just a moment, Rachel. (*Pauses, continuing slowly and very seriously*). Tom and Rachel! I have been trying to make up my mind for some time whether a certain thing is my duty or not. Today—I have decided it is. You are old enough, now,—and I see you ought to be told. Do you know what day this is? (*Both Tom and Rachel have been watching their mother intently*). It's the sixteenth of October. Does that mean anything to either of you?

TOM and RACHEL (*Wonderingly*): No.

MRS. LOVING (*Looking at both of them thoughtfully, half to herself*): No—I don't know why it should. (*Slowly*) Ten years ago—today—your father and your half-brother died.

TOM: I do remember, now, that you told us it was in October.

RACHEL (*With a sigh*): That explains—today.

MRS. LOVING: Yes, Rachel. (*Pauses*). Do you know—how they—died?

TOM and RACHEL: Why, no.

MRS. LOVING: Did it ever strike you as strange—that they —died— the same day?

TOM: Well, yes.

RACHEL: We often wondered, Tom and I; but—but somehow we never quite dared to ask you. You—you—always refused to talk about them, you know, Ma dear.

Mrs. Loving: Did you think—that—perhaps—the reason—I—I—wouldn't talk about them—was—because, because—I was ashamed—of them? (*Tom and Rachel look uncomfortable*).

Rachel: Well, Ma dear—we—we—did—wonder.

Mrs. Loving (*Questioningly*): And you thought?

Rachel (*Haltingly*): W-e-l-l—

Mrs. Loving (*Sharply*): Yes?

Tom: Oh! come, now, Rachel, you know we haven't bothered about it at all. Why should we? We've been happy.

Mrs. Loving: But when you have thought—you've been ashamed? (*Intensely*) Have you?

Tom: Now, Ma, aren't you making a lot out of nothing?

Mrs. Loving (*Slowly*): No. (*Half to herself*) You evade—both—of you. You *have* been ashamed. And I never dreamed until today you *could* take it this way. How blind—how almost criminally blind, I have been.

Rachel (*Tremulously*): Oh! Ma dear, don't! (*Tom and Rachel watch their mother anxiously and uncomfortably. Mrs. Loving is very evidently nerving herself for something*).

Mrs. Loving (*Very slowly, with restrained emotion*): Tom—and Rachel!

Tom: Ma!

Rachel: Ma dear! (*A tense, breathless pause*).

Mrs. Loving (*Bracing herself*): They — they — were lynched!!

Tom and Rachel (*In a whisper*): Lynched!

Mrs. Loving (*Slowly, laboring under strong but restrained emotion*): Yes—by Christian people—in a Christian land. We found out afterwards they were all church members in good standing—the best people. (*A silence*). Your father was a man among men. He was a fanatic. He was a Saint!

TOM (*Breathing with difficulty*): Ma—can you—will you—tell us—about it?

MRS. LOVING: I believe it to be my duty. (*A silence*). When I married your father I was a widow. My little George was seven years old. From the very beginning he worshiped your father. He followed him around—just like a little dog. All children were like that with him. I myself have never seen anybody like him. "Big" seems to fit him better than any other word. He was big-bodied—big-souled. His loves were big and his hates. You can imagine, then, how the wrongs of the Negro—ate into his soul. (*Pauses*). He was utterly fearless. (*A silence*). He edited and owned, for several years, a small negro paper. In it he said a great many daring things. I used to plead with him to be more careful. I was always afraid for him. For a long time, nothing happened—he was too important to the community. And then—one night—ten years ago—a mob made up of the respectable people in the town lynched an innocent black man—and what was worse—they knew him to be innocent. A white man was guilty. I never saw your father so wrought up over anything: he couldn't eat; he couldn't sleep; he brooded night and day over it. And then—realizing fully the great risk he was running, although I begged him not to—and all his friends also—he deliberately and calmly went to work and published a most terrific denunciation of that mob. The old prophets in the Bible were not more terrible than he. A day or two later, he received an anonymous letter, very evidently from an educated man, calling upon him to retract his words in the next issue. If he refused his life was threatened. The next week's issue contained an arraignment as frightful, if not more so, than the previous one. Each word was white-hot, searing. That night, some dozen masked men came to our house.

RACHEL (*Moaning*): Oh, Ma dear! Ma dear!

MRS. LOVING (*Too absorbed to hear*): We were not asleep —your father and I. They broke down the front door and made their way to our bedroom. Your father kissed me—and took up his revolver. It was always loaded. They broke down the door. (*A silence. She continues slowly and quietly*) I tried to shut my eyes—I could not. Four masked men fell—they did not move any more—after a little. (*Pauses*). Your father was finally overpowered and dragged out. In the hall—my little seventeen-year-old George tried to rescue him. Your father begged him not to interfere. He paid no attention. It ended in their dragging them both out. (*Pauses*). My little George—was—a man! (*Controls herself with an effort*). He never made an outcry. His last words to me were: "Ma, I am glad to go with Father." I could only nod to him. (*Pauses*). While they were dragging them down the steps, I crept into the room where you were. You were both asleep. Rachel, I remember, was smiling. I knelt down by you—and covered my ears with my hands—and waited. I could not pray—I couldn't for a long time—afterwards. (*A silence*). It was very still when I finally uncovered my ears. The only sounds were the faint rustle of leaves and the "tap-tapping of the twig of a tree" against the window. I hear it still—sometimes in my dreams. *It was the tree—where they were.* (*A silence*). While I had knelt there waiting—I had made up my mind what to do. I dressed myself and then I woke you both up and dressed you. (*Pauses*). We set forth. It was a black, still night. Alternately dragging you along and carrying you—I walked five miles to the house of some friends. They took us in, and we remained there until I had seen my dead laid comfortably at rest. They lent me money to come North—I couldn't bring you up—in the South. (*A silence*). Always remember this: There never lived anywhere—or at any time—any two whiter or more beautiful souls. God gave me one for a husband and one for a son and I am proud. (*Brokenly*) You—must—be—proud—too. (*A long silence. Mrs. Loving bows her head in her hands. Tom controls himself with an effort. Rachel creeps softly to her mother, kneels beside her and lifts the hem of her dress to her lips. She does not dare touch her. She adores her with her eyes*).

MRS. LOVING (*Presently raising her head and glancing at the clock*): Tom, it's time, now, for you to go to work. Rachel and I will finish up here.

TOM (*Still laboring under great emotion goes out into the entryway and comes back and stands in the doorway with his cap. He twirls it around and around nervously*): I want you to know, Ma, before I go—how—how proud I am. Why, I didn't believe two people could be like that —and live. And then to find out that one—was your own father—and one—your own brother.—It's wonderful! I'm—not much yet, Ma, but—I've—I've just got to be something now. (*Breaks off*). (*His face becomes distorted with passion and hatred*). When I think— when I think—of those devils with white skins—living somewhere today—living and happy—I—see—red! I— I—goodbye! (*Rushes out, the door bangs*).

MRS. LOVING (*Half to herself*): I was afraid—of just that. I wonder—if I did the wise thing—after all.

RACHEL (*With a gesture infinitely tender, puts her arms around her mother*): Yes, Ma dear, you did. And, here-after, Tom and I share and share alike with you. To think, Ma dear, of ten years of this—all alone. It's wicked! (*A short silence*).

MRS. LOVING: And, Rachel, about that dear, little boy, Jimmy.

RACHEL: Now, Ma dear, tell me tomorrow. You've stood enough for one day.

MRS. LOVING: No, it's better over and done with—all at once. If I had seen that dear child suddenly any other day than this—I might have borne it better. When he lifted his little face to me—and smiled—for a moment— I thought it was the end—of all things. Rachel, he is the image of my boy—my George!

RACHEL: Ma dear!

MRS. LOVING: And, Rachel—it will hurt—to see him again.

RACHEL: I understand, Ma dear. (*A silence. Suddenly*) Ma dear, I am beginning to see—to understand—so much. (*Slowly and thoughtfully*) Ten years ago, all things being equal, Jimmy might have been—George? Isn't that so?

MRS. LOVING: Why—yes, if I understand you.

RACHEL:I guess that doesn't sound very clear. It's only getting clear to me, little by little. Do you mind my thinking out loud to you?

MRS. LOVING: No, chickabiddy.

RACHEL: If Jimmy went South now—and grew up—he might be—a George?

MRS. LOVING: Yes.

RACHEL: Then, the South is full of tens, hundreds, thousands of little boys, who, one day may be—and some of them with certainty—Georges?

MRS. LOVING: Yes, Rachel.

RACHEL: And the little babies, the dear, little, helpless babies, being born today—now—and those who will be, tomorrow, and all the tomorrows to come—have *that* sooner or later to look forward to? They will laugh and play and sing and be happy and grow up, perhaps, and be ambitious—just for *that?*

MRS. LOVING: Yes, Rachel.

RACHEL: Then, everywhere, everywhere, throughout the South, there are hundreds of dark mothers who live in fear, terrible, suffocating fear, whose rest by night is broken, and whose joy by day in their babies on their hearts is three parts—pain. Oh, I know this is true—for this is the way I should feel, if I were little Jimmy's mother. How horrible! Why—it would be more merciful—to strangle the little things at birth. And so this nation—this white Christian nation—has deliberately set its curse upon the most beautiful—the most holy thing in life—motherhood! Why—it—makes—you doubt—God!

MRS. LOVING: Oh, hush! little girl. Hush!

RACHEL (*Suddenly with a great cry*): Why, Ma dear, *you know. You* were a *mother, George's mother.* So, this is what it means. Oh, Ma dear! Ma dear! (*Faints in her mother's arms*).

ACT II.

TIME: *October sixteenth, four years later; seven o'clock in the morning.*

SCENE: *The same room. There have been very evident improvements made. The room is not so bare; it is cosier. On the shelf, before each window, are potted red geraniums. At the windows are green denim drapery curtains covering fresh white dotted Swiss inner curtains. At each doorway are green denim portieres. On the wall between the kitchenette and the entrance to the outer rooms of the flat, a new picture is hanging, Millet's "The Man With the Hoe." Hanging against the side of the run that faces front is Watts's "Hope." There is another easy-chair at the left front. The table in the center is covered with a white table-cloth. A small asparagus fern is in the middle of this. When the curtain rises there is the clatter of dishes in the kitchenette. Presently Rachel enters with dishes and silver in her hands. She is clad in a bungalow apron. She is noticeably all of four years older. She frowns as she sets the table. There is a set expression about the mouth. A child's voice is heard from the rooms within.*

JIMMY (*Still unseen*): Ma Rachel!

RACHEL (*Pauses and smiles*): What is it, Jimmy boy?

JIMMY (*Appearing in rear doorway, half-dressed, breathless, and tremendously excited over something. Rushes toward Rachel*): Three guesses! Three guesses! Ma Rachel!

RACHEL (*Her whole face softening*): Well, let's see—maybe there is a circus in town.

JIMMY: No siree! (*In a sing-song*) You're not right! You're not right!

RACHEL: Well, maybe Ma Loving's going to take you somewhere.

JIMMY: No! (*Vigorously shaking his head*) It's—

RACHEL (*Interrupting quickly*) You said I could have three guesses, honey. I've only had two.

JIMMY: I thought you had three. How many are three?

RACHEL (*Counting on her fingers*): One! Two! Three! I've only had one! two!—See? Perhaps Uncle Tom is going to give you some candy.

JIMMY (*Dancing up and down*): No! No! No! (*Catches his breath*) I leaned over the bath-tub, way over, and got hold of the chain with the button on the end, and dropped it into the little round place in the bottom. And then I runned lots and lots of water in the tub and climbed over and fell in splash! just like a big stone; (*Loudly*) and took a bath all by myself alone.

RACHEL (*Laughing and hugging him*): All by yourself, honey? You ran the water, too, boy, not "runned" it. What I want to know is, where was Ma Loving all this time?

JIMMY: I stole in "creepy-creep" and looked at Ma Loving and she was awful fast asleep. (*Proudly*) Ma Rachel, I'm a "nawful," big boy now, aren't I? I are almost a man, aren't I?

RACHEL: Oh! Boy, I'm getting tired of correcting you—"I am almost a man, am I not?" Jimmy, boy, what will Ma Rachel do, if you grow up? Why, I won't have a little boy any more! Honey, you mustn't grow up, do you hear? You mustn't.

JIMMY: Oh, yes, I must; and you'll have me just the same, Ma Rachel. I'm going to be a policeman and make lots of money for you and Ma Loving and Uncle Tom, and I'm going to buy you some trains and fire-engines, and little, cunning ponies, and some rabbits, and some great 'normous banks full of money—lots of it. And then, we are going to live in a great, big castle and eat lots of ice cream, all the time, and drink lots and lots of nice pink lemonade.

RACHEL: What a generous Jimmy boy! (*Hugs him*). Before I give you "morning kiss," I must see how clean my boy is. (*Inspects teeth, ears and neck*). Jimmy, you're sweet and clean enough to eat. (*Kisses him; he tries to strangle her with hugs*). Now the hands. Oh! Jimmy, look at those nails! Oh! Jimmy! (*Jimmy wriggles and tries to get his hands away*). Honey, get my file off of my bureau and go to Ma Loving; she must be awake by this time. Why, honey, what's the matter with your feet?

JIMMY. I don't know. I thought they looked kind of queer, myself. What's the matter with them?

RACHEL (*Laughing*): You have your shoes on the wrong feet.

JIMMY (*Bursts out laughing*): Isn't that most 'normously funny? I'm a case, aren't I—(*pauses thoughtfully*) I mean—am I nŏt, Ma Rachel?

RACHEL: Yes, honey, a great big case of molasses. Come, you must hurry now, and get dressed. You don't want to be late for school, you know.

JIMMY: Ma Rachel! (*Shyly*) I—I have been making something for you all the morning—ever since I waked up. It's awful nice. It's—stoop down, Ma Rachel, please— a great, big (*puts both arms about her neck and gives her a noisy kiss. Rachel kisses him in return, then pushes his head back. For a long moment they look at each other; and, then, laughing joyously, he makes believe he is a horse, and goes prancing out of the room. Rachel, with a softer, gentler expression, continues setting the table. Presently, Mrs. Loving, bent and worn-looking, appears in the doorway in the rear. She limps a trifle.*)

MRS. LOVING: Good morning, dearie. How's my little girl, this morning? (*Looks around the room*). Why, where's Tom? I was certain I heard him running the water in the tub, sometime ago. (*Limps into the room*).

RACHEL (*Laughing*): Tom isn't up yet. Have you seen Jimmy?

MRS. LOVING: Jimmy? No. I didn't know he was awake, even.

RACHEL (*Going to her mother and kissing her*): Well! What do you think of that! I sent the young gentleman to you, a few minutes ago, for help with his nails. He is very much grown up this morning, so I suppose that explains why he didn't come to you. Yesterday, all day, you know, he was a puppy. No one knows what he will be by tomorrow. All of this, Ma dear, is preliminary to telling you that Jimmy boy has stolen a march on you, this morning.

MRS. LOVING: Stolen a march! How?

RACHEL: It appears that he took his bath all by himself and, as a result, he is so conceited, peacocks aren't in it with him.

MRS. LOVING: I heard the water running and thought, of course, it was Tom. Why, the little rascal! I must go and see how he has left things. I was just about to wake him up.

RACHEL: Rheumatism's not much better this morning, Ma dear. (*Confronting her mother*) Tell me the truth, now, did you or did you not try that liniment I bought you yesterday?

34

Mrs. Loving (*Guiltily*): Well, Rachel, you see—it was this way, I was—I was so tired, last night,—I—I really forgot it.

Rachel: I thought as much. Shame on you!

Mrs. Loving: As soon as I walk around a bit it will be all right. It always is. It's bad, when I first get up—that's all. I'll be spry enough in a few minutes. (*Limps to the door; pauses*) Rachel, I don't know why the thought should strike me, but how very strangely things turn out. If any one had told me four years ago that Jimmy would be living with us, I should have laughed at him. Then it hurt to see him; now it would hurt not to. (*Softly*) Rachel, sometimes—I wonder—if, perhaps, God—hasn't relented a little—and given me back my boy,—my George.

Rachel: The whole thing was strange, wasn't it?

Mrs. Loving: Yes, God's ways are strange and often very beautiful; perhaps all would be beautiful—if we only understood.

Rachel: God's ways are certainly very mysterious. Why, of all the people in this apartment-house, should Jimmy's father and mother be the only two to take the smallpox, and the only two to die. It's queer!

Mrs. Loving: It doesn't seem like two years ago, does it?

Rachel: Two years, Ma dear! Why it's three the third of January.

Mrs. Loving: Are you sure, Rachel?

Rachel (*Gently*): I don't believe I could ever forget that, Ma dear.

Mrs. Loving: No, I suppose not. That is one of the differences between youth and old age—youth attaches tremendous importance to dates,—old age does not.

Rachel (*Quickly*): Ma dear, don't talk like that. You're not old.

MRS. LOVING: Oh! yes, I am, dearie. It's sixty long years since I was born; and I am much older than that, much older.

RACHEL: Please, Ma dear, please!

MRS. LOVING (*Smiling*): Very well, dearie, I won't say it any more. (*A pause*). By the way,—how—does Tom strike you, these days?

RACHEL (*Avoiding her mother's eye*): The same old, bantering, cheerful Tom. Why?

MRS. LOVING: I know he's all that, dearie, but it isn't possible for him to be really cheerful. (*Pauses; goes on wistfully*) When you are little, we mothers can kiss away all the trouble, but when you grow up—and go out—into the world—and get hurt—we are helpless. There is nothing we can do.

RACHEL: Don't worry about Tom, Ma dear, he's game. He doesn't show the white feather.

MRS. LOVING: Did you see him, when he came in, last night?

RACHEL: Yes.

MRS. LOVING: Had he had—any luck?

RACHEL: No. (*Firmly*) Ma dear, we may as well face it— it's hopeless, I'm afraid.

MRS. LOVING: I'm afraid—you are right. (*Shakes her head sadly*) Well, I'll go and see how Jimmy has left things and wake up Tom, if he isn't awake yet. It's the waking up in the mornings that's hard. (*Goes limping out rear door. Rachel frowns as she continues going back and forth between the kitchenette and the table. Presently Tom appears in the door at the rear. He watches Rachel several moments before he speaks or enters. Rachel looks grim enough*).

TOM (*Entering and smiling*): Good-morning, "Merry Sunshine"! Have you, perhaps, been taking a—er—prolonged draught of that very delightful beverage—vinegar? (*Rachel, with a knife in her hand, looks up unsmiling. In pretended fright*) I take it all back, I'm sure. May I request, humbly, that before I press my chaste, morning salute upon your forbidding lips, that you—that you—that you—er—in some way rid yourself of that—er—knife? (*Bows as Rachel puts it down*). I thank you. (*He comes to her and tips her head back; gently*) What's the matter with my little Sis?

RACHEL (*Her face softening*) : Tommy dear, don't mind me. I'm getting wicked, I guess. At present I feel just like——like curdled milk. Once upon a time, I used to have quite a nice disposition, didn't I, Tommy?

TOM (*Smiling*) : Did you, indeed! I'm not going to flatter you. Well, brace yourself, old lady. Ready, One! Two! Three! Go! (*Kisses her, then puts his hands on either side of her face, and raising it, looks down into it*). You're a pretty, decent little sister, Sis, that's what T. Loving thinks about it; and he knows a thing or two. (*Abruptly looking around*) Has the paper come yet?

RACHEL : I haven't looked, it must have, though, by this time. (*Tom, hands in his pockets, goes into the vestibule. He whistles. The outer door opens and closes, and presently he saunters back, newspaper in hand. He lounges carelessly in the arm-chair and looks at Rachel*).

TOM : May T. Loving be of any service to you?

RACHEL : Service! How?

TOM : May he run, say, any errands, set the table, cook the breakfast? Anything?

RACHEL (*Watching the lazy figure*) : You look like working.

TOM (*Grinning*) : It's at least—polite—to offer.

RACHEL : You can't do anything; I don't trust you to do it right. You may just sit there, and read your paper—and try to behave yourself.

Tom (*In affectedly meek tones*): Thank you, ma'am. (*Opens the paper, but does not read. Jimmy presently enters riding around the table on a cane. Rachel peeps in from the kitchenette and smiles. Tom puts down his paper*). 'Lo! Big Fellow, what's this?

Jimmy (*Disgustedly*): How can I hear? I'm miles and miles away yet. (*Prances around and around the room; presently stops near Tom, attempting a gruff voice*) Good-morning!

Tom (*Lowering his paper again*): Bless my stars! Who's this? Well, if it isn't Mr. Mason! How-do-you-do, Mr. Mason? That's a beautiful horse you have there. He limps a trifle in his left, hind, front foot, though.

Jimmy: He doesn't!

Tom: He does!

Jimmy (*Fiercely*): He doesn't!

Tom (*As fiercely*): I say he does!

Mrs. Loving (*Appearing in the doorway in the rear*): For Heaven's sake! What is this? Good-morning, Tommy.

Tom (*Rising and going toward his mother, Jimmy following astride of the cane in his rear*): Good-morning, Ma. (*Kisses her; lays his head on her shoulder and makes believe he is crying; in a high falsetto*) Ma! Jimmy says his horse doesn't limp in his hind, front right leg, and I say he does.

Jimmy (*Throws his cane aside, rolls on the floor and kicks up his heels. He roars with laughter*): I think Uncle Tom is funnier than any clown in the "Kickus."

Tom (*Raising his head and looking down at Jimmy; Rachel stands in the kitchenette doorway*): In the *what*, Jimmy?

Jimmy: In the "kickus," of course.

Tom: "Kickus"! "Kickus"! Oh, Lordy! (*Tom and Rachel shriek with laughter; Mrs. Loving looks amused; Jimmy, very much affronted, gets upon his feet again.*

Tom leans over and swings Jimmy high in the air). Boy, you'll be the death of me yet. Circus, son! Circus!

JIMMY (*From on high, soberly and with injured dignity*): Well, I thinks "Kickus" and circus are very much alike. Please put me down.

RACHEL (*From the doorway*): We laugh, honey, because we love you so much.

JIMMY (*Somewhat mollified, to Tom*): Is that so, Uncle Tom?

TOM: Surest thing in the world! (*Severely*) Come, get down, young man. Don't you know you'll wear my arms out? Besides, there is something in my lower vest pocket, that's just dying to come to you. Get down, I say.

JIMMY (*Laughing*): How can I get down? (*Wriggles around*).

TOM: How should I know? Just get down, of course. (*Very suddenly puts Jimmy down on his feet. Jimmy tries to climb up over him*).

JIMMY: Please sit down, Uncle Tom?

TOM (*In feigned surprise*): Sit down! What for?

JIMMY (*Pummeling him with his little fists, loudly*): Why, you said there was something for me in your pocket.

TOM (*Sitting down*): So I did. How forgetful I am!

JIMMY (*Finding a bright, shiny penny, shrieks*): Oh! Oh! Oh! (*Climbs up and kisses Tom noisily*).

TOM: Why, Jimmy! You embarrass me. My! My!

JIMMY: What is 'barrass?

TOM: You make me blush.

JIMMY: What's that?

MRS. LOVING: Come, come, children! Rachel has the breakfast on the table. (*Tom sits in Jimmy's place and Jimmy tries to drag him out*).

TOM: What's the matter, now?

JIMMY: You're in *my* place.

Tom : Well, can't you sit in mine?

Jimmy (*Wistfully*) : I wants to sit by my Ma Rachel.

Tom : Well, so do I.

Rachel : Tom, stop teasing Jimmy. Honey, don't you let him bother you; ask him please prettily.

Jimmy : Please prettily, Uncle Tom.

Tom : Oh! well then. (*Gets up and takes his own place. They sit as they did in Act I. only Jimmy sits between Tom, at the end, and Rachel*).

Jimmy (*Loudly*) : Oh, goody! goody! goody! We've got sau-sa-ges.

Mrs. Loving : Sh!

Jimmy (*Silenced for a few moments; Rachel ties a big napkin around his neck, and prepares his breakfast. He breaks forth again suddenly and excitedly*) : Uncle Tom!

Tom : Sir?

Jimmy : I took a bath this morning, all by myself alone, in the bath-tub, and I ranned, no (*Doubtfully*) I runned, I think—the water all in it, and got in it all by myself; and Ma Loving thought it was you; but it was *me*.

Tom (*In feignedly severe tones*) : See here, young man, this won't do. Don't you know I'm the only one who is allowed to do that here? It's a perfect waste of water —that's what it is.

Jimmy (*Undaunted*) : Oh! no, you're not the only one, 'cause Ma Loving and Ma Rachel and me—alls takes baths every single morning. So, there!

Tom : You 'barrass me. (*Jimmy opens his mouth to ask a question; Tom quickly*) Young gentleman, your mouth is open. Close it, sir; close it.

Mrs. Loving : Tom, you're as big a child exactly as Jimmy.

Tom (*Bowing to right and left*) : You compliment me. I thank you, I am sure.

(*They finish in silence.*)

JIMMY (*Sighing with contentment*): I'm through, Ma Rachel.

MRS. LOVING: Jimmy, you're a big boy, now, aren't you? (*Jimmy nods his head vigorously and looks proud.*) I wonder if you're big enough to wash your own hands, this morning?

JIMMY (*Shrilly*): Yes, ma'am.

MRS. LOVING: Well, if they're beautifully clean, I'll give you another penny.

JIMMY (*Excitedly to Rachel*): Please untie my napkin, Ma Rachel! (*Rachel does so.*) "Excoose" me, please.

MRS. LOVING AND RACHEL: Certainly. (*Jimmy climbs down and rushes out at the rear doorway.*)

MRS. LOVING (*Solemnly and slowly; breaking the silence*): Rachel, do you know what day this is?

RACHEL (*Looking at her plate; slowly*): Yes, Ma dear.

MRS. LOVING: Tom.

TOM (*Grimly and slowly*): Yes, Ma.

(*A silence.*)

MRS. LOVING (*Impressively*): We must never—as long—as we live—forget this day.

RACHEL: No, Ma dear.

TOM: No, Ma.

(*Another silence*)

TOM (*Slowly; as though thinking aloud*): I hear people talk about God's justice—and I wonder. There, are you, Ma. There isn't a sacrifice—that you haven't made. You're still working your fingers to the bone—sewing— just so all of us may keep on living. Rachel is a graduate in Domestic Science; she was high in her class; most of the girls below her in rank have positions in the schools. I'm an electrical engineer—and I've tried steadily for several months—to practice my profession. It seems our educations aren't of much use to us: we aren't allowed to make good—because our skins are dark. (*Pauses*) And, in the South today, there are white men —(*Controls himself*). They have everything; they're well-dressed, well-fed, well-housed; they're prosperous in business; they're important politically; they're pillars in the church. I know all this is true—I've inquired. Their children (our ages, some of them) are growing up around them; and they are having a square deal handed out to them—college, position, wealth, and best of all, freedom, without galling restrictions, to work out their own salvations. With ability, they may become— anything; and all this will be true of their children's children after them. (*A pause*). Look at us—and look at them. We are destined to failure—they, to success. Their children shall grow up in hope; ours, in despair. Our hands are clean;—theirs are red with blood—red with the blood of a noble man—and a boy. They're nothing but low, cowardly, bestial murderers. The scum of the earth shall succeed. —God's justice, I suppose.

MRS. LOVING (*Rising and going to Tom; brokenly*): Tom, promise me—one thing.

TOM (*Rises gently*): What is it, Ma?

MRS. LOVING: That—you'll try—not to lose faith—in God. I've been where you are now—and it's black. Tom, we don't understand God's ways. My son, I know, now— He is beautiful. Tom, won't you try to believe, again?

TOM (*Slowly, but not convincingly*): I'll try, Ma.

MRS. LOVING (*Sighs*): Each one, I suppose, has to work out his own salvation. (*After a pause*) Rachel, if you'll get Jimmy ready, I'll take him to school. I've got to go down town shopping for a customer, this morning. (*Rachel rises and goes out the rear doorway; Mrs. Loving, limping very slightly now, follows. She turns and looks back yearningly at Tom, who has seated himself again, and is staring unseeingly at his plate. She goes out. Tom sits without moving until he hears Mrs. Loving's voice within and Rachel's faintly; then he gets the paper, sits in the arm-chair and pretends to read).*

MRS. LOVING (*From within*): A yard, you say, Rachel? You're sure that will be enough. Oh! you've measured it. Anything else?—What?—Oh! all right. I'll be back by one o'clock, anyway. Good-bye. (*Enters with Jimmy. Both are dressed for the street. Tom looks up brightly at Jimmy*).

TOM: Hello! Big Fellow, where are you taking *my* mother, I'd like to know? This is a pretty kettle of fish.

JIMMY (*Laughing*): Aren't you funny, Uncle Tom! Why, I'm not taking her anywhere. She's taking me. (*Importantly*) I'm going to school.

TOM: Big Fellow, come here. (*Jimmy comes with a rush*). Now, where's that penny I gave you? No, I don't want to see it. All right. Did Ma Loving give you another? (*Vigorous noddings of the head from Jimmy*). I wish you to promise me solemnly—Now, listen! Here, don't wriggle so! not to buy—Listen! too many pints of ice-cream with my penny. Understand?

JIMMY (*Very seriously*): Yes, Uncle Tom, cross my "tummy"! I promise.

TOM: Well, then, you may go. I guess that will be all for the present. (*Jimmy loiters around looking up wistfully into his face*). Well?

JIMMY: Haven't you—aren't you—isn't you—forgetting something?

TOM (*Grabbing at his pockets*): Bless my stars! what now?

JIMMY: If you could kind of lean over this way. (*Tom leans forward*). No, not that way. (*Tom leans toward the side away from Jimmy*). No, this way, this way!

(*Laughs and pummels him with his little fists*). This
way!

Tom (*Leaning toward Jimmy*) : Well, why didn't you say
so, at first?

Jimmy (*Puts his arms around Tom's neck and kisses him*) :
Good-bye, dear old Uncle Tom. (*Tom catches him and
hugs him hard*). I likes to be hugged like that—I can
taste—sau-sa-ges.

Tom : You 'barrass me, son. Here, Ma, take your boy. Now
remember all I told you, Jimmy.

Jimmy : I 'members.

Mrs. Loving : God bless you, Tom. Good luck.

Jimmy (*To Tom*) : God bless you, Uncle Tom. Good luck!

Tom (*Much affected, but with restraint, rising*) : Thank
you—Good-bye. (*Mrs. Loving and Jimmy go out through
the vestibule. Tom lights a cigarette and tries to read
the paper. He soon sinks into a brown study. Presently
Rachel enters humming. Tom relights his cigarette; and
Rachel proceeds to clear the table. In the midst of this,
the bell rings three distinct times*).

Rachel and Tom : John!

Tom : I wonder what's up—It's rather early for him.—I'll
go. (*Rises leisurely and goes out into the vestibule. The
outer door opens and shuts. Men's voices are heard.
Tom and John Strong enter. During the ensuing conversation Rachel finishes clearing the table, takes the
fern off, puts on the green table-cloth, places a doily carefully in the centre, and replaces the fern. She apparently
pays no attention to the conversation between her brother
and Strong. After she has finished, she goes to the
kitchenette. The rattle of dishes can be heard now and
then*).

RACHEL (*Brightly*): Well, stranger, how does it happen you're out so early in the morning?

STRONG: I hadn't seen any of you for a week, and I thought I'd come by, on my way to work, and find out how things are going. There is no need of asking how you are, Rachel. And the mother and the boy?

RACHEL: Ma dear's rheumatism still holds on. —Jimmy's fine.

STRONG: I'm sorry to hear that your mother is not well. There isn't a remedy going that my mother doesn't know about. I'll get her advice and let you know. (*Turning to Tom*) Well, Tom, how goes it? (*Strong and Tom sit*).

TOM (*Smiling grimly*): There's plenty of "go," but no "git there."   (*There is a pause*).

STRONG: I was hoping for better news.

TOM: If I remember rightly, not so many years ago, you tried—and failed. Then, a colored man had hardly a ghost of a show;—now he hasn't even the ghost of a ghost. (*Rachel has finished and goes into the kitchenette*).

STRONG: That's true enough. (*A pause*). What are you going to do?

TOM (*Slowly*): I'll do this little "going act" of mine the rest of the week; (*pauses*) and then, I'll do anything I can get to do. If necessary, I suppose, I can be a "White-wing."

STRONG: Tom, I came— (*Breaks off; continuing slowly*) Six years ago, I found I was up against a stone wall— your experience, you see, to the letter. I couldn't let my mother starve, so I became a waiter. (*Pauses*). I studied waiting; I made a science of it, an art. In a comparatively short time, I'm a head-waiter and I'm up against another stonewall. I've reached my limit. I'm thirty-two now, and I'll die a head-waiter. (*A pause*).

College friends, so-called, and acquaintances used to come into the restaurant. One or two at first—attempted to commiserate with me. They didn't do it again. I waited upon them—I did my best. Many of them tipped me. (*Pauses and smiles grimly*). I can remember my first tip, still. They come in yet; many of them are already powers, not only in this city, but in the country. Some of them make a personal request that I wait upon them. I am an artist, now, in my proper sphere. They tip me well, extremely well—the larger the tip, the more pleased they are with me. Because of me, in their own eyes, they're philanthropists. Amusing, isn't it? I can stand their attitude now. My philosophy—learned hard, is to make the best of everything you can, and go on. At best, life isn't so very long. You're wondering why I'm telling you all this. I wish you to see things exactly as they are. There are many disadvantages and some advantages in being a waiter. My mother can live comfortably; I am able, even, to see that she gets some of the luxuries. Tom, it's this way—I can always get you a job as a waiter; I'll teach you the art. If you care to begin the end of the week—all right. And remember this, as long as I keep my job—this offer holds good.

TOM: I—I— (*Breaks off*) Thank you. (*A pause; then smiling wryly*) I guess it's safe enough to say, you'll see me at the end of the week. John you're— (*Breaking off again. A silence interrupted presently by the sound of much vigorous rapping on the outer door of the flat. Rachel appears and crosses over to the vestibule*). Hear the racket! My kiddies gently begging for admittance. It's about twenty minutes of nine, isn't it? (*Tom nods*). I thought so. (*Goes into the entryway; presently reappears with a group of six little girls ranging in age from five to about nine. All are fighting to be close to her; and all are talking at once. There is one exception: the smallest tot is self-possessed and self-sufficient. She carries a red geranium in her hand and gives it her full attention).*

LITTLE MARY: It's my turn to get "Morning kiss" first, this morning, Miss Rachel. You kissed Louise first yesterday. You said you'd kiss us "alphebettically." *(Ending in a shriek).* You promised! *(Rachel kisses Mary, who subsides).*

LITTLE NANCY *(Imperiously)*: Now, me. *(Rachel kisses her, and then amid shrieks, recriminations, pulling of hair, jostling, etc., she kisses the rest. The small tot is still oblivious to everything that is going on).*

RACHEL *(Laughing)*: You children will pull me limb from limb; and then I'll be all dead; and you'll be sorry—see, if you aren't. *(They fall back immediately. Tom and John watch in amused silence. Rachel loses all self-consciousness, and seems to bloom in the children's midst).* Edith! come here this minute, and let me tie your hair-ribbon again. Nancy, I'm ashamed of you, I saw you trying to pull it off. *(Nancy looks abashed but mischievous).* Louise, you look as sweet as sweet, this morning; and Jenny, where did you get the pretty, pretty dress?

LITTLE JENNY *(Snuffling, but proud)*: My mother made it. *(Pauses with more snuffles).* My mother says I have a very bad cold. *(There is a brief silence interruped by the small tot with the geranium).*

LITTLE MARTHA *(In a sweet, little voice)*: I—have—a—pitty—'ittle flower.

RACHEL: Honey, it's beautiful. Don't you want "Morning kiss" too?

LITTLE MARTHA: Yes, I do.

RACHEL: Come, honey. (*Rachel kisses her*). Are you going to give the pretty flower to Jenny's teacher: (*Vigorous shakings of the head in denial*). Is it for—mother? (*More shakings of the head*). Is it for—let's see—Daddy? (*More shakings of the head*). I give up. To whom are you going to give the pretty flower, honey?

LITTLE MARTHA (*Shyly*): "Oo."

RACHEL: You, darling!

LITTLE MARTHA: Muzzer and I picked it—for "oo." Here 't is. (*Puts her finger in her mouth, and gives it shyly*).

RACHEL: Well, I'm going to pay you with three big kisses. One! Two! Three!

LITTLE MARTHA: I can count, One! Two! Free! Tan't I? I am going to school soon; and I wants to put the flower in your hair.

RACHEL (*Kneels*): All right, baby. (*Little Martha fumbles and Rachel helps her*).

LITTLE MARTHA (*Dreamily*): Miss Rachel, the 'ittle flower loves you. It told me so. It said it wanted to lie in your hair. It is going to tell you a pitty 'ittle secret. You listen awful hard—and you'll hear. I wish I were a fairy and had a little wand, I'd turn everything into flowers. Wouldn't that be nice, Miss Rachel?

RACHEL: Lovely, honey!

LITTLE JENNY (*Snuffling loudly*): If I were a fairy and had a wand, I'd turn you, Miss Rachel, into a queen—and then I'd always be near you and see that you were happy.

RACHEL: Honey, how beautiful!

LITTLE LOUISE: I'd make my mother happy—if I were a fairy. She cries all the time. My father can't get anything to do.

LITTLE NANCY: If I were a fairy, I'd turn a boy in my school into a spider. I hate him.

RACHEL: Honey, why?

LITTLE NANCY: I'll tell you sometime—I hate him.

LITTLE EDITH: Where's Jimmy, Miss Rachel?

RACHEL: He went long ago; and chickies, you'll have to clear out, all of you, now, or you'll be late. Shoo! Shoo! (*She drives them out prettily before her. They laugh merrily. They all go into the vestibule*).

TOM (*Slowly*): Does it ever strike you—how pathetic and tragic a thing—a little colored child is?

STRONG: Yes.

TOM: Today, we colored men and women, everywhere—are up against it. Every year, we are having a harder time of it. In the South, they make it as impossible as they can for us to get an education. We're hemmed in on all sides. Our one safeguard—the ballot—in most states, is taken away already, or is being taken away. Economically, in a few lines, we have a slight show—but at what a cost! In the North, they make a pretence of liberality: they give us the ballot and a good education, and then—snuff us out. Each year, the problem just to live, gets more difficult to solve. How about these children—if we're fools enough to have any? (RACHEL *re-enters. Her face is drawn and pale. She returns to the kitchenette.*)

STRONG (*Slowly, with emphasis*): That part—is damnable! (*A silence.*)

TOM (*Suddenly looking at the clock*): It's later than I thought. I'll have to be pulling out of here now, if you don't mind. (*Raising his voice*) Rachel! (*Rachel still drawn and pale, appears in the doorway of the kitchenette. She is without her apron*). I've got to go now, Sis. I leave John in your hands.

STRONG: I've got to go, myself, in a few minutes.

TOM: Nonsense, man! Sit still. I'll begin to think, in a minute, you're afraid of the ladies.

STRONG: I am.

TOM: What! And not ashamed to acknowledge it?

STRONG: No.

TOM: You're lots wiser than I dreamed. So long! (*Gets hat out in the entry-way and returns; smiles wryly.*) "Morituri Salutamus". (*They nod at him—Rachel wistfully. He goes out. There is the sound of an opening and closing door. Rachel sits down. A rather uncomfortable silence, on the part of Rachel, ensues. Strong is imperturbable.*)

RACHEL (*Nervously*): John!

STRONG: Well?

RACHEL: I—I listened.

STRONG: Listened! To what?

RACHEL: To you and Tom.

STRONG: Well,—what of it?

RACHEL: I didn't think it was quite fair not to tell you. It—it seemed, well, like eavesdropping.

STRONG: Don't worry about it. Nonsense!

RACHEL: I'm glad—I want to thank you for what you did for Tom. He needs you, and will need you. You'll help him?

STRONG: (*Thoughtfully*): Rachel, each one—has his own little battles. I'll do what I can. After all, an outsider doesn't help much.

RACHEL: But friendship—just friendship—helps.

STRONG: Yes. (*A silence*). Rachel, do you hear anything encouraging from the schools? Any hope for you yet?

RACHEL: No, nor ever will be. I know that now. There's no more chance for me than there is for Tom,—or than there was for you—or for any of us with dark skins. It's lucky for me that I love to keep house, and cook, and sew. I'll never get anything else. Ma dear's sewing, the little work Tom has been able to get, and the little

50

sewing I sometimes get to do—keep us from the poor-house. We live. According to your philosophy, I suppose, make the best of it—it might be worse.

STRONG (*Quietly*): You don't want to get morbid over these things, you know.

RACHEL (*Scornfully*): That's it. If you see things as they are, you're either pessimistic or morbid.

STRONG: In the long run, do you believe, that attitude of mind—will be—beneficial to you? I'm ten years older than you. I tried your way. I know. Mine is the only sane one. (*Goes over to her slowly; deliberately puts his hands on her hair, and tips her head back. He looks down into her face quietly without saying anything*).

RACHEL (*Nervous and startled*): Why, John, don't! (*He pays no attention, but continues to look down into her face*).

STRONG (*Half to himself*): Perhaps—if you had—a little more fun in your life, your point of view would be—more normal. I'll arrange it so I can take you to some theatre, one night, this week.

RACHEL (*Irritably*): You talk as though I were a—a jelly-fish. You'll take me, how do you know *I'll* go?

STRONG: You will.

RACHEL (*Sarcastically*): Indeed! (STRONG *makes no reply*). I wonder if you know how—how—maddening you are. Why, you talk as though my will counts for nothing. It's as if you're trying to master me. I think a domineering man is detestable.

STRONG (*Softly*): If he's, perhaps, *the* man?

RACHEL (*Hurriedly, as though she had not heard*): Besides, some of these theatres put you off by yourself as though you had leprosy. I'm not going.

STRONG (*Smiling at her*): You know I wouldn't ask you to go, under those circumstances. (*A silence*). Well, I must be going now. (*He takes her hand, and looks at it reverently. Rachel, at first resists; but he refuses to let go. When she finds it useless, she ceases to resist. He turns his head and smiles down into her face*). Rachel, I am coming back to see you, this evening.

RACHEL: I'm sure *we'll* all be very glad to see you.

STRONG (*Looking at her calmly*): I said—*you*. (*Very deliberately, he turns her hand palm upwards, leans over and kisses it; then he puts it back into her lap. He touches her cheek lightly*). Good-bye—little Rachel. (*Turns in the vestibule door and looks back, smiling*). Until tonight. (*He goes out. Rachel sits for some time without moving. She is lost in a beautiful day-dream. Presently she sighs happily, and after looking furtively around the room, lifts the palm John has kissed to her lips. She laughs shyly and jumping up, begins to hum. She opens the window at the rear of the room and then commences to thread the sewing-machine. She hums happily the whole time. A light rapping is heard at the outer door. Rachel listens. It stops, and begins again. There is something insistent, and yet hopeless in the sound. Rachel looking puzzled, goes out into the vestibule...The door closes. Rachel, a black woman, poorly dressed, and a little ugly, black child come in. There is the stoniness of despair in the woman's face. The child is thin, nervous, suspicious, frightened*).

MRS. LANE (*In a sharp, but toneless voice*): May I sit down? I'm tired.

RACHEL (*Puzzled, but gracious; draws up a chair for her*): Why, certainly.

MRS. LANE: No, you don't know me—never even heard of me—nor I of you. I was looking at the vacant flat on this floor—and saw your name—on your door,—"Loving!" It's a strange name to come across—in this world. —I thought, perhaps, you might give me some information. (*The child hides behind her mother and looks around at Rachel in a frightened way*).

RACHEL (*Smiling at the woman and child in a kindly manner*): I'll be glad to tell you anything, I am able Mrs.—

MRS. LANE: Lane. What I want to know is, how do they treat the colored children in the school I noticed around the corner? (*The child clutches at her mother's dress*).

RACHEL (*Perplexed*): Very well—I'm sure.

MRS. LANE (*Bluntly*): What reason have you for being sure?

RACHEL: Why, the little boy I've adopted goes there; and he's very happy. All the children in this apartment-house go there too; and I know they're happy.

MRS. LANE: Do you know how many colored children there are in the school?

RACHEL: Why, I should guess around thirty.

MRS. LANE: I see. (*Pauses*). What color is this little adopted boy of yours?

RACHEL (*Gently*): Why—he's brown.

MRS. LANE: Any black children there?

RACHEL (*Nervously*): Why—yes.

MRS. LANE: Do you mind if I send Ethel over by the piano to sit?

RACHEL: N—no, certainly not. (*Places a chair by the piano and goes to the little girl holding out her hand. She smiles beautifully. The child gets farther behind her mother*).

MRS. LANE: She won't go to you—she's afraid of everybody now but her father and me. Come Ethel. (*Mrs. Lane takes the little girl by the hand and leads her to the chair. In a gentler voice*) Sit down, Ethel. (*Ethel obeys.*

When her mother starts back again toward Rachel, she holds out her hands pitifully. She makes no sound). I'm not going to leave you, Ethel. I'll be right over here. You can see me. *(The look of agony on the child's face, as her mother leaves her, makes Rachel shudder).* Do you mind if we sit over here by the sewing-machine? Thank you. *(They move their chairs).*

RACHEL *(Looking at the little, pitiful figure watching its mother almost unblinkingly)* : Does Ethel like apples, Mrs. Lane?

MRS. LANE: Yes.

RACHEL: Do you mind if I give her one?

MRS. LANE: No. Thank you, very much.

RACHEL *(Goes into the kitchenette and returns with a fringed napkin, a plate, and a big, red apple, cut into quarters. She goes to the little girl, who cowers away from her; very gently).* Here, dear, little girl, is a beautiful apple for you. *(The gentle tones have no appeal for the trembling child before her).*

MRS. LANE *(Coming forward)* : I'm sorry, but I'm afraid she won't take it from you. Ethel, the kind lady has given you an apple. Thank her nicely. Here! I'll spread the napkin for you, and put the plate in your lap. Thank the lady like a good little girl.

ETHEL *(Very low)* : Thank you. *(They return to their seats. Ethel with difficulty holds the plate in her lap. During the rest of the interview between Rachel and her mother, she divides her attention between the apple on the plate and her mother's face. She makes no attempt to eat the apple, but holds the plate in her lap with a care that is painful to watch. Often, too, she looks over her shoulder fearfully. The conversation between Rachel and her mother is carried on in low tones).*

MRS. LANE: I've got to move—it's *Ethel.*

RACHEL: What is the matter with that child? It's—it's heartbreaking to see her.

MRS. LANE: I understand how you feel,—I don't feel anything, myself, any more. (*A pause*). My husband and I are poor, and we're ugly and we're black. Ethel looks like her father more than she does like me. We live in 55th Street—near the railroad. It's a poor neighborhood, but the rent's cheap. My husband is a porter in a store; and, to help out, I'm a caretaker. (*Pauses*). I don't know why I'm telling you all this. We had a nice little home— and the three of us were happy. Now we've got to move.

RACHEL: Move! Why?

MRS. LANE: It's Ethel. I put her in school this September. She stayed two weeks. (*Pointing to Ethel*) That's the result.

RACHEL (*In horror*): You mean—that just two weeks—in school—did that?

MRS. LANE: Yes. Ethel never had a sick day in her life— before. (*A brief pause*). I took her to the doctor at the end of the two weeks. He says she's a nervous wreck.

RACHEL: But what could they have done to her?

MRS. LANE (*Laughs grimly and mirthlessly*): I'll tell you what they did the first day. Ethel is naturally sensitive and backward. She's not assertive. The teacher saw that, and, after I had left, told her to sit in a seat in the rear of the class. She was alone there—in a corner. The children, immediately feeling there was something wrong with Ethel because of the teacher's attitude, turned and stared at her. When the teacher's back was turned they whispered about her, pointed their fingers at her and tittered. The teacher divided the class into two parts, divisions, I believe, they are called. She forgot all about Ethel, of course, until the last minute, and then, looking back, said sharply: "That little girl there may join this division," meaning the group of pupils standing around her. Ethel naturally moved slowly. The teacher called her sulky and told her to lose a part of her recess. When Ethel came up—the children drew away from her in every direction. She was left standing alone. The teacher then proceeded to give a lesson about kindness to animals. Funny, isn't it, *kindness* to *animals?* The children forgot Ethel in the excitement of talking about their pets. Presently, the teacher turned to Ethel and said disagreeably: "Have you a pet?" Ethel said, "Yes," very low. "Come, speak up, you sulky child, what is it?" Ethel said: "A blind puppy." They all laughed, the teacher and all. Strange, isn't it, but Ethel loves that puppy. She spoke up: "It's mean to laugh at a little blind puppy. I'm glad he's blind." This remark brought forth more laughter. "Why are you glad," the teacher asked curiously. Ethel refused to say. (*Pauses*). When I asked her why, do you know what she told me? "If he saw me, he might not love me any more." (*A pause*). Did I tell you that Ethel is only seven years old?

RACHEL (*Drawing her breath sharply*): Oh! I didn't believe any one could be as cruel as that—to a little child.

MRS. LANE: It isn't very pleasant, is it? When the teacher found out that Ethel wouldn't answer, she said severely: "Take your seat!" At recess, all the children went out. Ethel could hear them playing and laughing and shrieking. Even the teacher went too. She was made to sit there all alone—in that big room—because God made her ugly —and black. (*Pauses*). When the recess was half over the teacher came back. "You may go now," she said coldly. Ethel didn't stir. "Did you hear me?" "Yes'm." "Why don't you obey?" "I don't want to go out, please." "You don't, don't you, you stubborn child! Go immediately!" Ethel went. She stood by the school steps.

No one spoke to her. The children near her moved away in every direction. They stopped playing, many of them, and watched her. They stared as only children can stare. Some began whispering about her. Presently one child came up and ran her hand roughly over Ethel's face. She looked at her hand and Ethel's face and ran screaming back to the others, "It won't come off! See!" Other children followed the first child's example. Then one boy spoke up loudly: "I know what she is, she's a nigger!" Many took up the cry. God or the devil interfered—the bell rang. The children filed in. One boy boldly called her "Nigger!" before the teacher. She said, "That isn't nice,"—but she smiled at the boy. Things went on about the same for the rest of the day. At the end of school, Ethel put on her hat and coat—the teacher made her hang them at a distance from the other pupils' wraps; and started for home. Quite a crowd escorted her. They called her "Nigger!" all the way. I *made* Ethel go the next day. I complained to the authorities. They treated me lightly. I was determined not to let them force my child out of school. At the end of two weeks—I had to take her out.

RACHEL (*Brokenly*): Why,—I never—in all my life— heard anything—so—pitiful.

MRS. LANE: Did you ever go to school here?

RACHEL: Yes. I was made to feel my color—but I never had an experience like that.

MRS. LANE: How many years ago were you in the graded schools?

RACHEL: Oh!—around ten.

MRS. LANE (*Laughs grimly*): Ten years! Every year things are getting worse. Last year wasn't as bad as this. (*Pauses.*) So they treat the children all right in this school?

RACHEL: Yes! Yes! I know that.

MRS. LANE: I can't afford to take this flat here, but I'll take it. I'm going to have Ethel educated. Although, when you think of it,—it's all rather useless—this education! What are our children going to do with it, when they get it? We strive and save and sacrifice to educate them—and the whole time—down underneath, we know —they'll have no chance.

RACHEL (Sadly): Yes, that's true, all right.—God seems to have forgotten us.

MRS. LANE: God! It's all a lie about God. I know.—This fall I sent Ethel to a white Sunday-school near us. She received the same treatment there she did in the day school. Her being there, nearly broke up the school. At the end, the superintendent called her to him and asked her if she didn't know of some nice colored Sunday-school. He told her she must feel out of place, and uncomfortable there. That's your Church of God!

RACHEL: Oh! how unspeakably brutal. (Controls herself with an effort; after a pause) Have you any other children?

MRS. LANE (Dryly): Hardly! If I had another—I'd kill it. It's kinder. (Rising presently) Well, I must go, now. Thank you, for your information—and for listening. (Suddenly) You aren't married, are you?

RACHEL: No.

MRS. LANE: Don't marry—that's my advice. Come, Ethel. (Ethel gets up and puts down the things in her lap, carefully upon her chair. She goes in a hurried, timid way to her mother and clutches her hand). Say good-bye to the lady.

ETHEL (Faintly): Good-bye.

RACHEL (Kneeling by the little girl—a beautiful smile on her face) Dear little girl, won't you let me kiss you

58

good-bye? I love little girls. (*The child hides behind her mother; continuing brokenly*) Oh!—no child—ever did—that to me—before!

MRS. LANE (*In a gentler voice*) : Perhaps, when we move in here, the first of the month, things may be better. Thank you, again. Good-morning! You don't belie your name. (*All three go into the vestibule. The outside door opens and closes. Rachel as though dazed and stricken returns. She sits in a chair, leans forward, and clasping her hands loosely between her knees, stares at the chair with the apple on it where Ethel Lane has sat. She does not move for some time. Then she gets up and goes to the window in the rear center and sits there. She breathes in the air deeply and then goes to the sewing-machine and begins to sew on something she is making. Presently her feet slow down on the pedals; she stops; and begins brooding again. After a short pause, she gets up and begins to pace up and down slowly, mechanically, her head bent forward. The sharp ringing of the electric bell breaks in upon this. Rachel starts and goes slowly into the vestibule. She is heard speaking dully through the tube*).

RACHEL: Yes!—All right! Bring it up! (*Presently she returns with a long flower box. She opens it listlessly at the table. Within are six, beautiful crimson rosebuds with long stems. Rachel looks at the name on the card. She sinks down slowly on her knees and leans her head against the table. She sighs wearily*) Oh! John! John!—What are we to do?—I'm—I'm—afraid! Every-where—it is the same thing. My mother! My little brother! Little, black, crushed Ethel! (*In a whisper*) Oh! God! You who I have been taught to believe are so good, so beautiful how could—You permit—these—things? (*Pauses, raises her head and sees the rosebuds. Her face softens and grows beautiful, very sweetly*).

Dear little rosebuds—you—make me think—of sleeping, curled up, happy babies. Dear beautiful, little rosebuds! (*Pauses; goes on thoughtfully to the rosebuds*) When—I look—at you—I believe—God is beautiful. He who can make a little exquisite thing like this, and this can't be cruel. Oh! He can't mean me—to give up—love—and the hope of little children. (*There is the sound of a small hand knocking at the outer door. Rachel smiles*). My Jimmy! It must be twelve o'clock. (*Rises*). I didn't dream it was so late. (*Starts for the vestibule*). Oh! the world can't be so bad. I don't believe it. I won't. I *must* forget that little girl. My little Jimmy is happy—and today John—sent me beautiful rosebuds. Oh, there are lovely things, yet. (*Goes into the vestibule. A child's eager cry is heard; and Rachel carrying Jimmy in her arms comes in. He has both arms about her neck and is hugging her. With him in her arms, she sits down in the armchair at the right front*).

RACHEL: Well, honey, how was school today?

JIMMY (*Sobering a trifle*): All right, Ma Rachel. (*Suddenly sees the roses*) Oh! look at the pretty flowers. Why, Ma Rachel, you forgot to put them in water. They'll die.

RACHEL: Well, so they will. Hop down this minute, and I'll put them in right away. (*Gathers up box and flowers and goes into the kitchenette. Jimmy climbs back into the chair. He looks thoughtful and serious. Rachel comes back with the buds in a tall, glass vase. She puts the fern on top of the piano, and places the vase in the centre of the table*). There, honey, that's better, isn't it? Aren't they lovely?

JIMMY: Yes, that's lots better. Now they won't die, will they? Rosebuds are just like little "chilyun," aren't they, Ma Rachel? If you are good to them, they'll grow up into lovely roses, won't they? And if you hurt them, they'll die. Ma Rachel do you think all peoples are kind to little rosebuds?

RACHEL (*Watching Jimmy shortly*): Why, of course. Who could hurt little children? Who would have the heart to do such a thing?

JIMMY: If you hurt them, it would be lots kinder, wouldn't it, to kill them all at once, and not a little bit and a little bit?

RACHEL (*Sharply*): Why, honey boy, why are you talking like this?

JIMMY: Ma Rachel, what is a "Nigger"?

(*Rachel recoils as though she had been struck*).

RACHEL: Honey boy, why—why do you ask that?

JIMMY: Some big boys called me that when I came out of school just now. They said: "Look at the little nigger!" And they laughed. One of them runned, no ranned, after me and threw stones; and they all kept calling "Nigger! Nigger! Nigger!" One stone struck me hard in the back, and it hurt awful bad; but I didn't cry, Ma Rachel. I wouldn't let them make me cry. The stone hurts me there, Ma Rachel; but what they called me hurts and hurts here. What is a "Nigger," Ma Rachel?

RACHEL (*Controlling herself with a tremendous effort. At last she sweeps down upon him and hugs and kisses him*): Why, honey boy, those boys didn't mean anything. Silly, little, honey boy! They're rough, that's all. How *could* they mean anything?

JIMMY: You're only saying that, Ma Rachel, so I won't be hurt. I know. It wouldn't ache here like it does—if they didn't mean something.

RACHEL (*Abruptly*): Where's Mary, honey?

JIMMY: She's in her flat. She came in just after I did.

RACHEL: Well, honey, I'm going to give you two big cookies and two to take to Mary; and you may stay in there and play with her, till I get your lunch ready. Won't that be jolly?

JIMMY (*Brightening a little*): Why, you never give me but one at a time. You'll give me two?—One? Two? (*Rachel gets the cookies and brings them to him. Jimmy climbs down from the chair*). Shoo! now, little honey boy. See how many laughs you can make for me, before I come after you. Hear? Have a good time, now. (*Jimmy starts for the door quickly; but he begins to slow down. His face gets long and serious again. Rachel watches him*).

RACHEL (*Jumping at him*): Shoo! Shoo! Get out of here quickly, little chicken. (*She follows him out. The outer door opens and shuts. Presently she returns. She looks old and worn and grey; calmly. Pauses*). First, it's little, black Ethel—and then's it's Jimmy. Tomorrow, it will be some other little child. The blight—sooner or later—strikes all. My little Jimmy, only seven years old poisoned! (*Through the open window comes the laughter of little children at play. Rachel, shuddering, covers her ears*). And once I said, centuries ago, it must have been: "How can life be so terrible, when there are little children in the world?" Terrible! Terrible! (*In a whisper, slowly*) That's the reason it *is* so terrible. (*The laughter reaches her again; this time she listens*). And, suddenly, some day, from out of the black, the blight shall descend, and shall still forever—the laughter on those little lips, and in those little hearts. (*Pauses thoughtfully*). And the loveliest thing—almost, that ever happened to me, that beautiful voice, in my dream, those beautiful words: "Rachel, you are to be the mother to little children. (*Pauses, then slowly and with dawning surprise*). Why, God, you were making a mock of me; you were laughing at me. I didn't belive God could laugh at our sufferings, but He can. We are accursed, accursed! We have nothing, absolutely nothing. (*Strong's rosebuds attract her attention. She goes over to them, puts her hand out as if to touch them, and then shakes her head, very sweetly*) No, little rosebuds, I may not touch you. Dear, little, baby rosebuds,—I am accursed. (*Gradually her whole form stiffens, she breathes deeply; at last slowly*). You God!—You terrible, laughing God! Listen! I swear—and may my soul be damned to all eternity, if I do break this oath—I swear—that no child of mine shall ever lie upon my breast, for I will not have it rise up, in the terrible days that are to be—and call me cursed. (*A pause, very wistfully; questioningly*). Never to know the loveliest thing in all the world—the feel of a little head, the touch of little hands, the beautiful utter dependence—of a little child? (*With sudden frenzy*) You can laugh, Oh God! Well, so can I. (*Bursts into terrible, racking laughter*) But I can be kinder than You. (*Fiercely she snatches the rosebuds from the vase, grasps them roughly, tears each head from the stem, and grinds it under her feet. The vase goes over with a crash; the water drips unheeded over the table-cloth and floor*). If I kill, You Mighty God, I kill at once—I do not torture. (*Falls face downward on the floor. The laughter of the children shrills loudly through the window*).

ACT III.

TIME: *Seven o'clock in the evening, one week later.*

PLACE: *The same room. There is a coal fire in the grate. The curtains are drawn. A lighted oil lamp with a dark green porcelain shade is in the center of the table. Mrs. Loving and Tom are sitting by the table, Mrs. Loving sewing, Tom reading. There is the sound of much laughter and the shrill screaming of a child from the bedrooms. Presently Jimmy clad in a flannelet sleeping suit, covering all of him but his head and hands, chases a pillow, which has come flying through the doorway at the rear. He struggles with it, finally gets it in his arms, and rushes as fast as he can through the doorway again. Rachel jumps at him with a cry. He drops the pillow and shrieks. There is a tussle for possession of it, and they disappear. The noise grows louder and merrier. Tom puts down his paper and grins. He looks at his mother.*

TOM: Well, who's the giddy one in this family now?

MRS. LOVING (*Shaking her head in a troubled manner*): I don't like it. It worries me. Rachel—(*Breaks off*).

TOM: Have you found out, yet—

MRS. LOVING (*Turning and looking toward the rear doorway, quickly interrupting him*): Sh! (*Rachel, laughing, her hair tumbling over her shoulders, comes rushing into the room. Jimmy is in close pursuit. He tries to catch her, but she dodges him. They are both breathless*).

65

MRS. LOVING (*Deprecatingly*): Really, Rachel, Jimmy will be so excited he won't be able to sleep. It's after his bedtime, now. Don't you think you had better stop?

RACHEL: All right, Ma dear. Come on, Jimmy; let's play "Old Folks" and sit by the fire. (*She begins to push the big armchair over to the fire. Tom jumps up, moves her aside, and pushes it himself. Jimmy renders assistance.*]

TOM: Thanks, Big Fellow, you are "sure some" strong. I'll remember you when these people around here come for me to move pianos and such things around. Shake! (*They shake hands*).

JIMMY (*Proudly*): I am awful strong, am I not?

TOM: You "sure" are a Hercules. (*Hurriedly, as Jimmy's mouth and eyes open wide*). And see here! don't ask me tonight who that was. I'll tell you the first thing tomorrow morning. Hear? (*Returns to his chair and paper*).

RACHEL (*Sitting down*): Come on, honey boy, and sit in my lap.

JIMMY (*Doubtfully*): I thought we were going to play "Old Folks."

RACHEL: We are.

JIMMY: Do old folks sit in each other's laps?

RACHEL: Old folks do anything. Come on.

JIMMY (*Hesitatingly climbs into her lap, but presently snuggles down and sighs audibly from sheer content; Rachel starts to bind up her hair*): Ma Rachel, don't please! I like your hair like that. You're—you're pretty. I like to feel of it; and it smells like—like—oh!—like a barn.

RACHEL: My! how complimentary! I like that. Like a barn, indeed!

JIMMY: What's "complimentry"?

RACHEL: Oh! saying nice things about me. (*Pinching his cheek and laughing*) That my hair is like a barn, for instance.

JIMMY (*Stoutly*): Well, that is "complimentary." It smells like hay—like the hay in the barn you took me to, one day, last summer. 'Member?

RACHEL: Yes honey.

JIMMY (*After a brief pause*): Ma Rachel!

RACHEL: Well?

JIMMY: Tell me a story, please. It's "story-time," now, isn't it?

RACHEL: Well, let's see. (*They both look into the fire for a space; beginning softly*) Once upon a time, there were two, dear, little boys, and they were all alone in the world. They lived with a cruel, old man and woman, who made them work hard, very hard—all day, and beat them when they did not move fast enough, and always, every night, before they went to bed. They slept in an attic on a rickety, narrow bed, that went screech! screech! whenever they moved. And, in summer, they nearly died with the heat up there, and in winter, with the cold. One wintry night, when they were both weeping very bitterly after a particularly hard beating, they suddenly heard a pleasant voice saying: "Why are you crying, little boys?" They looked up, and there, in the moonlight, by their bed, was the dearest, little old lady. She was dressed all in gray, from the peak of her little pointed hat to her little, buckled shoes. She held a black cane much taller than her little self. Her hair fell about her ears in tiny, grey corkscrew curls, and they bobbed about as she moved. Her eyes were black and bright—as bright as—well, as that lovely, white light there. No, there! And her cheeks were as red as the apple I gave you yesterday. Do you remember?

JIMMY (*Dreamily*): Yes.

RACHEL: "Why are you crying, little boys?" she asked again, in a lovely, low, little voice. "Because we are tired and sore and hungry and cold; and we are all alone in the world; and we don't know how to laugh any more. We should so like to laugh again." "Why, that's easy," she said, "it's just like this." And she laughed a little, joyous, musical laugh. "Try!" she commanded. They tried, but their laughing boxes were very rusty, and they made horrid sounds. "Well," she said, "I advise you to pack up, and go away, as soon as you can, to the Land of Laughter. You'll soon learn there, I can tell you." "Is there such a land?" they asked doubtfully. "To be sure there is," she answered the least bit sharply. "We never heard of it," they said. "Well, I'm sure there must be plenty of things you never heard about," she said just the "leastest" bit more sharply. "In a moment you'll be telling me flowers don't talk together, and the birds." "We never heard of such a thing," they said in surprise, their eyes like saucers. "There!" she said, bobbing her little curls. "What did I tell you? You have much to learn." "How do you get to the Land of Laughter?" they asked. "You go out of the eastern gate of the town, just as the sun is rising; and you take the highway there, and follow it; and if you go with it long enough, it will bring you to the very gates of the Land of Laughter. It's a long, long way from here; and it will take you many days." The words had scarcely left her mouth, when, lo! the little lady disappeared, and where she had stood was the white square of moonlight—nothing else. And without more ado these two little boys put their arms around each other and fell fast asleep. And in the grey, just before daybreak, they awoke and dressed; and, putting on their ragged caps and mittens, for it was a wintry day, they stole out of the house and made for the eastern gate. And just as they reached it, and passed through, the whole east leapt into fire. All day they walked, and many days thereafter, and kindly people, by the way, took them in and gave them food and drink and sometimes a bed at night. Often they slept by the roadside, but they didn't mind that for the climate was delightful—not too hot, and not too cold. They soon threw away their ragged little mittens. They walked for many days, and there was no Land of Laughter. Once they met an old man, richly dressed, with shining jewels on his fingers, and he stopped them and asked: "Where are you going so fast, little boys?" "We are going to the Land of Laughter," they said together gravely. "That," said the old man, "is a very foolish thing to do. Come with me, and I will take you to the Land of Riches. I will cover you with garments of beauty, and give you jewels and a castle to live in and servants and horses and many things besides." And they said to him: "No, we wish to learn how to laugh again; we have forgotten how, and we are going to the Land of Laughter." "You will regret not going with me. See, if you don't," he said; and he left them in quite a huff. And they walked again, many days, and again they met an old man. He was tall and imposing-looking and very dignified. And he said: "Where are you going so fast, little boys?" "We are going to the Land of Laughter," they said together very seriously. "What!" he said, "that is an extremely foolish thing to do. Come with me, and I will give you power. I will make you great men: generals, kings, emperors, Whatever you desire to accomplish will be permitted you." And they smiled politely: "Thank you very much, but we have forgotten how to laugh, and we are going there to learn how." He looked upon them haughtily, without speaking, and disappeared. And they walked and walked more days; and they met another old man. And he was clad in rags, and his face was thin, and his eyes were unhappy. And he whispered to them: "Where are you going so fast, little boys?" "We are going to the Land of Laughter," they answered, without a smile. "Laughter! Laughter! that is useless. Come with me and I will show you the beauty of life through sacrifice, suffering for others. That is the only life. I come from the Land of Sacrifice." And they thanked him kindly, but said: "We have suffered long enough. We have forgotten how to laugh. We would learn again." And they went on; and he looked after them very wistfully. They walked more days, and at last they came to the Land of Laughter. And how do you suppose they knew this? Because they could hear, over the wall, the sound of joyous laughter,— the laughter of men, women, and children. And one sat guarding the gate, and they went to her. "We have come a long, long distance; and we would enter the Land of Laughter." "Let me see you smile, first," she said gently. "I sit at the gate; and no one who does not know how to smile may enter the Land of Laughter." And they tried to smile, but could not. "Go away and practice," she said kindly, "and come back tomorrow." And they went away, and practiced all night how to smile; and in the morning they returned, and the gentle lady at the gate said: "Dear little boys, have you learned how to smile?" And they said: "We have tried. How is this?" "Better," she said, "much better. Practice some more, and come back tomorrow." And they went away obediently and practiced. And they came the third day. And she said: "Now try again." And tears of delight came into her lovely eyes. "Those were very beautiful smiles," she said. "Now, you may enter." And she unlocked the gate, and kissed them both, and they entered the Land—the beautiful Land of Laughter. Never had they seen such blue skies, such green trees and grass; never had they heard such birds songs. And people, men, women and children, laughing softly, came to meet them, and took them in, and made them as home; and soon, very soon, they learned to sleep. And they grew up here, and married, and had laughing, happy children. And sometimes they thought of the Land of Riches, and said: "Ah! well!" and sometimes of the Land of Power, and sighed a little; and sometimes of the Land of Sacrifice—and their eyes were wistful. But they soon forgot, and laughed again. And they grew old, laughing. And then when they died —a laugh was on their lips. Thus are things in the beautiful Land of Laughter. (*There is a long pause*).

JIMMY: I like that story, Ma Rachel. It's nice to laugh, isn't is? Is there such a land?

RACHEL (*Softly*): What do you think, honey?

JIMMY: I thinks it would be awful nice if there was. Don't you?

RACHEL (*Wistfully*): If there only were! If there only were!

JIMMY: Ma Rachel.

RACHEL: Well?

JIMMY: It makes you think—kind of—doesn't it—of sunshine medicine?

RACHEL: Yes, honey,—but it isn't medicine there. It's always there—just like—well—like our air here. It's *always* sunshine there.

JIMMY: Always sunshine? Never any dark?

RACHEL: No, honey.

JIMMY: You'd—never—be—afraid there, then, would you? Never afraid of nothing?

RACHEL: No, honey.

JIMMY (*With a big sigh*): Oh!—Oh! I *wisht* it was here— not there. (*Puts his hand up to Rachel's face; suddenly sits up and looks at her*). Why, Ma Rachel dear, you're crying. Your face is all wet. Why! Don't cry! Don't cry!

RACHEL (*Gently*) : Do you remember that I told you the lady at the gate had tears of joy in her eyes, when the two, dear, little boys smiled that beautiful smile?

JIMMY: Yes.

RACHEL: Well, these are tears of joy, honey, that's all— tears of joy.

JIMMY: It must be awful queer to have tears of joy, 'cause you're happy. I never did. (*With a sigh*). But, if you say they are, dear Ma Rachel, they must be. You knows everything, don't you?

RACHEL (*Sadly*) : Some things, honey, some things. (*A silence*).

JIMMY (*Sighing happily*) : This is the beautiful-est night I ever knew. If you would do just one more thing, it would be lots more beautiful. Will you, Ma Rachel?

RACHEL: Well, what, honey?

JIMMY: Will you sing—at the piano, I mean, it's lots prettier that way—the little song you used to rock me to sleep by? You know, the one about the "Slumber Boat"?

RACHEL: Oh! honey, not tonight. You're too tired. It's bedtime now.

JIMMY (*Patting her face with his little hand; wheedlingly*) : Please! Ma Rachel, please! pretty please!

RACHEL: Well, honey boy, this once, then. Tonight, you shall have the little song—I used to sing you to sleep by (*half to herself*) perhaps, for the last time.

JIMMY: Why, Ma Rachel, why the last time?

RACHEL (*Shaking her head sadly, goes to the piano; in a whisper*) : The last time. (*She twists up her hair into a knot at the back of her head and looks at the keys for a few moments; then she plays the accompaniment of the*

"Slumber Boat" through softly, and, after a moment, sings. Her voice is full of pent-up longing, and heartbreak, and hopelessness. She ends in a little sob, but attempts to cover it by singing, lightly and daintily, the chorus of "The Owl and the Moon."..Then softly and with infinite tenderness, almost against her will, she plays and sings again the refrain of the "Slumber Boat"):

> "Sail, baby, sail
>   Out from that sea,
> Only don't forget to sail
>   Back again to me."

(Presently she rises and goes to Jimmy, who is lolling back happily in the big chair. During the singing, Tom and Mrs. Loving apparently do not listen; when she sobs, however, Tom's hand on his paper tightens; Mrs. Loving's needle poises for a moment in mid-air. Neither looks at Rachel. Jimmy evidently has not noticed the sob).

RACHEL *(Kneeling by Jimmy)* : Well, honey, how did you like it?

JIMMY *(Proceeding to pull down her hair from the twist)* : It was lovely, Ma Rachel. *(Yawns audibly).* Now, Ma Rachel, I'm just beautifully sleepy. *(Dreamily)* I think that p'r'aps I'll go to the Land of Laughter tonight in my dreams. I'll go in the "Slumber Boat" and come back in the morning and tell you all about it. Shall I?

RACHEL: Yes, honey. *(Whispers)*

> "Only don't forget to sail
>   Back again to me."

TOM *(Suddenly)* : Rachel! *(Rachel starts slightly).* I nearly forgot. John is coming here tonight to see how you are. He told me to tell you so.

RACHEL (*Stiffens perceptibly, then in different tones*) : Very well. Thank you. (*Suddenly with a little cry she puts her arms around Jimmy*) Jimmy! honey! don't go tonight. Don't go without Ma Rachel. Wait for me, honey. I do so wish to go, too, to the Land of Laughter. Think of it, Jimmy; nothing but birds always singing, and flowers always blooming, and skies always blue—and people, all of them, always laughing, laughing. You'll wait for Ma Rachel, won't you, honey?

JIMMY: Is there really and truly, Ma Rachel, a Land of Laughter?

RACHEL: Oh! Jimmy, let's hope so; let's pray so.

JIMMY (*Frowns*) : I've been thinking— (*Pauses*). You have to smile at the gate, don't you, to get in?

RACHEL: Yes, honey.

JIMMY: Well, I guess I couldn't smile if my Ma Rachel wasn't somewhere close to me. So I couldn't get in after all, could I? Tonight, I'll go somewhere else, and tell you all about it. And then, some day, we'll go together, won't we?

RACHEL (*Sadly*) : Yes, honey, some day—some day. (*A short silence*). Well, this isn't going to "sleepy-sleep," is it? Go, now, and say good-night to Ma Loving and Uncle Tom.

JIMMY (*Gets down obediently, and goes first to Mrs. Loving. She leans over, and he puts his little arms around her neck. They kiss; very sweetly*) : Sweet dreams! God keep you all the night!

MRS. LOVING: The sweetest of sweet dreams to you, dear little boy! Good-night! (*Rachel watches, unwatched, the scene. Her eyes are full of yearning*).

JIMMY (*Going to Tom, who makes believe he does not see him*) : Uncle Tom!

Tom (*Jumps as though tremendously startled; Jimmy laughs*): My! how you frightened me. You'll put my gizzard out of commission, if you do that often. Well, sir, what can I do for you?

Jimmy: I came to say good-night.

Tom (*Gathering Jimmy up in his arms and kissing him; gently and with emotion*) Good-night, dear little Big Fellow! Good-night!

Jimmy: Sweet dreams! God keep you all the night! (*Goes sedately to Rachel, and holds out his little hand*). I'm ready, Ma Rachel. (*Yawns*) I'm so nice and sleepy.

Rachel (*With Jimmy's hand in hers, she hesitates a moment, and then approaches Tom slowly. For a short time she stands looking down at him; suddenly leaning over him*): Why, Tom, what a pretty tie! Is it new?

Tom: Well, no, not exactly. I've had it about a month. It is rather a beauty, isn't it?

Rachel: Why, I never remember seeing it.

Tom (*Laughing*): I guess not. I saw to that.

Rachel: Stingy!

Tom: Well, I am—where my ties are concerned. I've had experience.

Rachel (*Tentatively*): Tom!

Tom: Well?

Rachel (*Nervously and wistfully*): Are you—will you—I mean, won't you be home this evening?

Tom: You've got a long memory, Sis. I've that engagement, you know. Why?

Rachel (*Slowly*): I forgot; so you have.

Tom: Why?

Rachel (*Hastily*): Oh! nothing—nothing. Come on, Jimmy boy, you can hardly keep those little peepers open, can you? Come on, honey. (*Rachel and Jimmy go out the rear doorway. There is a silence*).

Mrs. Loving (*Slowly, as though thinking aloud*): I try to make out what could have happened; but it's no use—I can't. Those four days, she lay in bed hardly moving, scarcely speaking. Only her eyes seemed alive. I never saw such a wide, tragic look in my life. It was as though her soul had been mortally wounded. But how? how? What could have happened?

Tom (*Quietly*): I don't know. She generally tells me everything; but she avoids me now. If we are alone in a room—she gets out. I don't know what it means.

Mrs. Loving: She will hardly let Jimmy out of her sight. While he's at school, she's nervous and excited. She seems always to be listening, but for what? When he returns, she nearly devours him. And she always asks him in a frightened sort of way, her face as pale and tense as can be: "Well, honey boy, how was school today?" And he always answers, "Fine, Ma Rachel, fine! I learned—"; and then he goes on to tell her everything that has happened. And when he has finished, she says in an uneasy sort of way: "Is—is that all?" And when he says "Yes," she relaxes and becomes limp. After a little while she becomes feverishly happy. She plays with Jimmy and the children more than ever she did—and she played a good deal, as you know. They're here, or she's with them. Yesterday, I said in remonstrance, when she came in, her face pale and haggard and black hollows under her eyes: "Rachel, remember you're just out of a sickbed. You're not well enough to go on like this." "I know," was all she would say, "but I've got to. I can't help myself. This part of their little lives must be happy —it just must be." (*Pauses*). The last couple of nights, Jimmy has awakened and cried most pitfully. She wouldn't let me go to him; said I had enough trouble, and she could quiet him. She never will let me know why he cries; but she stays with him, and soothes him until, at last, he falls asleep again. Every time she has come out like a rag; and her face is like a dead woman's. Strange isn't it, this is the first time we have ever been able to talk it over? Tom, what could have happened?

Tom: I don't know, Ma, but I feel, as you do; something terrible and sudden has hurt her soul; and, poor little thing, she's trying bravely to readjust herself to life again. (*Pauses, looks at his watch and then rises, and goes to her. He pats her back awkwardly*). Well, Ma, I'm going now. Don't worry too much. Youth, you, know, gets over things finally. It takes them hard, that's all—. At least, that's what the older heads tell us. (*Gets his hat and stands in the vestibule doorway*). Ma, you know, I begin with John tomorrow. (*With emotion*) I don't believe we'll ever forget John. Good-night! (*Exit. Mrs. Loving continues to sew. Rachel, her hair arranged, re-enters through the rear doorway. She is humming*).

Rachel: He's sleeping like a top. Aren't little children, Ma dear, the sweetest things, when they're all helpless and asleep? One little hand is under his cheek; and he's smiling. (*Stops suddenly, biting her lips. A pause*) Where's Tom?

Mrs. Loving: He went out a few minutes ago.

Rachel (*Sitting in Tom's chair and picking up his paper. She is exceedingly nervous. She looks the paper over rapidly; presently trying to make her tone casual*): Ma,— you—you—aren't going anywhere tonight, are you?

Mrs. Loving: I've got to go out for a short time about half-past eight. Mrs. Jordan, you know. I'll not be gone very long, though. Why?

Rachel: Oh! nothing particular. I just thought it would be cosy if we could sit here together the rest of the evening. Can't you—can't you go tomorrow?

MRS. LOVING: Why, I don't see how I can. I've made the engagement. It's about a new reception gown; and she's exceedingly exacting, as you know. I can't afford to lose her.

RACHEL: No, I suppose not. All right, Ma dear. (*Presently, paper in hand, she laughs, but not quite naturally*). Look! Ma dear! How is that for fashion, anyway? Isn't it the "limit"? (*Rises and shows her mother a picture in the paper. As she is in the act, the bell rings. With a startled cry*). Oh! (*Drops the paper, and grips her mother's hand*).

MRS. LOVING (*Anxiously*):Rachel, your nerves are right on edge; and your hand feels like fire. I'll have to see a doctor about you; and that's all there is to it.

RACHEL (*Laughing nervously, and moving toward the vestibule*). Nonsense, Ma dear! Just because I let out a whoop now and then, and have nice warm hands? (*Goes out, is heard talking through the tube*) Yes! (*Her voice emitting tremendous relief*). Oh! bring it right up! (*Appearing in the doorway*) Ma dear, did you buy anything at Goddard's today?

MRS. LOVING: Yes; and I've been wondering why they were so late in delivering it. I bought it early this morning. (*Rachel goes out again. A door opens and shuts. She reappears with a bundle*).

MRS. LOVING: Put it on my bed, Rachel, please. (*Exit Rachel rear doorway; presently returns empty-handed; sits down again at the table with the paper between herself and mother; sinks in a deep revery. Suddenly there is the sound of many loud knocks made by numerous small fists. Rachel drops the paper, and comes to a sitting posture, tense again. Her mother looks at her, but says nothing. Almost immediately Rachel relaxes*).

RACHEL: My kiddies! They're late, this evening. (*Goes out into the vestibule. A door opens and shuts. There is the shrill, excited sound of childish voices. Rachel comes in surrounded by the children, all trying to say something to her at once. Rachel puts her finger on her lip and points toward the doorway in the rear. They all quiet down. She sits on the floor in the front of the stage, and the children all cluster around her. Their conversation takes place in a half-whisper. As they enter they nod brightly at Mrs. Loving, who smiles in return*). Why so late, kiddies? It's long past "sleepy-time."

LITTLE NANCY: We've been playing "Hide and Seek," and having the mostest fun. We promised, all of us, that if we could play until half-past seven tonight we wouldn't make any fuss about going to bed at seven o'clock the rest of the week. It's awful hard to go. I *hate* to go to bed!

LITTLE MARY, LOUISE and EDITH: So do I! So do I! So do I!

LITTLE MARTHA: I don't. I love bed. My bed, after my muzzer tucks me all in, is like a nice warm bag. I just stick my nose out. When I lifts my head up I can see the light from the dining-room come in the door. I can hear my muzzer and fazzer talking nice and low; and then, before I know it, I'm fast asleep, and I dream pretty things, and in about a minute it's morning again. I love my little bed, and I love to dream.

LITTLE MARY (*Aggressively*): Well, I guess I love to dream too. I wish I could dream, though, without going to bed.

LITTLE NANCY: When I grow up, I'm never going to bed at night! (*Darkly*) You see.

LITTLE LOUISE: "Grown-ups" just love to poke their heads out of windows and cry, "Child'run, it's time for bed now; and you'd better hurry, too, I can tell you." They "sure" are queer, for sometimes when I wake up, it must be

79

about twelve o'clock, I can hear by big sister giggling and talking to some silly man. If it's good for me to go to bed early—I should think—

RACHEL (*Interrupting suddenly*): Why, where is my little Jenny? Excuse me, Louise dear.

LITTLE MARTHA: Her cold is awful bad. She coughs like this (*giving a distressing imitation*) and snuffles all the time. She can't talk out loud, and she can't go to sleep. Muzzer says she's fev'rish—I thinks that's what she says. Jenny says she knows she could go to sleep, if you would come and sit with her a little while.

RACHEL: I certainly will. I'll go when you do, honey.

LITTLE MARTHA (*Softly stroking Rachel's arm*): You're the very nicest "grown-up", (*loyally*) except my muzzer, of course, I ever knew. You knows all about little chil'-run and you can be one, although you're all grown up. I think you would make a lovely muzzer. (*To the rest of the children*) Don't you?

ALL (*In excited whispers*): Yes, I do.

RACHEL (*Winces, then says gently*): Come, kiddies, you must go now, or your mothers will blame me for keeping you. (*Rises, as do the rest. Little Martha puts her hand into Rachel's*). Ma dear, I'm going down to sit a little while with Jenny. I'll be back before you go, though. Come, kiddies, say good-night to my mother.

ALL (*Gravely*): Good-night! Sweet dreams! God keep you all the night.

MRS. LOVING: Good-night dears! Sweet dreams, all!

(*Exeunt Rachel and the children. Mrs. Loving continues to sew. The bell presently rings three distinct times. In a few moments, Mrs. Loving gets up and goes out into the vestibule. A door opens and closes. Mrs. Loving and John Strong come in. He is a trifle pale but his imperturbable self. Mrs. Loving,*

80

somewhat nervous, takes her seat and resumes her sewing. She motions Strong to a chair. He returns to the vestibule, leaves his hat, returns, and sits down).

STRONG: Well, how is everything?

MRS. LOVING: Oh! about the same, I guess. Tom's out. John, we'll never forget you—and your kindness.

STRONG: That was nothing. And Rachel?

MRS. LOVING: She'll be back presently. She went to sit with a sick child for a little while.

STRONG: And how is she?

MRS. LOVING: She's not herself yet, but I think she is better.

STRONG (*After a short pause*): Well, what *did* happen—exactly?

MRS. LOVING: That's just what I don't know.

STRONG: When you came home—you couldn't get in—was that it?

MRS. LOVING: Yes. (*Pauses*). It was just a week ago today. I was down town all the morning. It was about one o'clock when I got back. I had forgotten my key. I rapped on the door and then called. There was no answer. A window was open, and I could feel the air under the door, and I could hear it as the draught sucked it through. There was no other sound. Presently I made such a noise the people began to come out into the hall. Jimmy was in one of the flats playing with a little girl named Mary. He told me he had left Rachel here a short time before. She had given him four cookies, two for him and two for Mary, and had told him he could play with her until she came to tell him his lunch was ready. I saw he was getting frightened, so I got the little girl and her mother to keep him in their flat. Then, as no man was at home, I sent out for help. Three men broke the door down. (*Pauses*). We found Rachel unconscious, lying on her face. For a few minutes I thought she was dead. (*Pauses*). A vase had fallen over on the table and the water had dripped through the cloth and onto the floor. There had been flowers in it. When I left, there were no flowers here. What she could have done to them, I can't say. The long stems were lying everywhere, and the flowers had been ground into the floor. I could tell that they must have been roses from the stems. After we had put her to bed and called the doctor, and she had finally regained consciousness, I very naturally asked her what had happened. All she would say was, "Ma dear, I'm too—tired—please." For four days she lay in bed scarcely moving, speaking only when spoken to. That first day, when Jimmy came in to see her, she shrank away from him. We had to take him out, and comfort him as best we could. We kept him away, almost by force, until she got up. And, then, she was utterly miserable when he was out of her sight. What happened, I don't know. She avoids Tom, and she won't tell me. (*Pauses*). Tom and I both believe her soul has been hurt. The trouble isn't with her body. You'll find her highly nervous. Sometimes she is very much depressed; again she is feverishly gay—almost reckless. What do you think about it, John?

STRONG (*Who has listened quietly*): Had anybody been here, do you know?

MRS. LOVING: No, I don't. I don't like to ask Rachel; and I can't ask the neighbors.

STRONG: No, of course not. (*Pauses*). You say there were some flowers?

MRS. LOVING: Yes.

STRONG: And the flowers were ground into the carpet?

MRS. LOVING: Yes.

STRONG: Did you happen to notice the box? They must have come in a box, don't you think?

MRS. LOVING: Yes, there was a box in the kitchenette. It was from "Marcy's." I saw no card.

STRONG (*Slowly*): It is rather strange. (*A long silence, during which the outer door opens and shuts. Rachel is heard singing. She stops abruptly. In a second or two she appears in the door. There is an air of suppressed excitement about her*).

RACHEL: Hello! John. (*Strong rises, nods at her, and brings forward for her the big arm-chair near the fire*). I thought that was your hat in the hall. It's brand new, I know—but it looks—"Johnlike." How are you? Ma! Jenny went to sleep like a little lamb. I don't like her breathing, though. (*Looks from one to the other; flippantly*) Who's dead? (*Nods her thanks to Strong for the chair and sits down*).

MRS. LOVING: Dead, Rachel?

RACHEL: Yes. The atmosphere here is so funereal,—it's positively "crapey."

STRONG: I don't know why it should be—I was just asking how you are.

RACHEL: Heavens! Does the mere inquiry into my health precipitate such an atmosphere? Your two faces were as long, as long—(*Breaks off*). Kind sir, let me assure you, I am in the very best of health. And how are you, John?

STRONG: Oh! I'm always well. (*Sits down*).

MRS. LOVING: Rachel, I'll have to get ready to go now. John, don't hurry. I'll be back shortly, probably in three-quarters of an hour—maybe less.

RACHEL: And maybe more, if I remember Mrs. Jordan. However, Ma dear, I'll do the best I can—while you are away. I'll try to be a credit to your training. (*Mrs.*

Loving smiles and goes out the rear doorway). Now, let's see—in the books of etiquette, I believe, the properly reared young lady, always asks the young gentleman caller—you're young enough, aren't you, to be classed still as a "young gentleman caller?" (*No answer*). Well, anyway, she always asks the young gentleman caller sweetly something about the weather. (*Primly*) This has been an exceedingly beautiful day, hasn't it, Mr. Strong? (*No answer from Strong, who, with his head resting against the back of the chair, and his knees crossed is watching her in an amused, quizzical manner*). Well, really, every properly brought up young gentleman, I'm sure, ought to know, that it's exceedingly rude not to answer a civil question.

STRONG (*Lazily*) : Tell me what to answer, Rachel.

RACHEL : Say, "Yes, very"; and look interested and pleased when you say it.

STRONG (*With a half-smile*) : Yes, very.

RACHEL : Well, I certainly wouldn't characterize that as a particularly animated remark. Besides, when you look at me through half-closed lids like that—and kind of smile—what are you thinking? (*No answer*) John Strong, are you deaf or—just plain stupid?

STRONG : Plain stupid, I guess.

RACHEL (*In wheedling tones*) : What were you thinking, John?

STRONG (*Slowly*) : I was thinking—(*Breaks off*)

RACHEL (*Irritably*) : Well?

STRONG : I've changed my mind.

RACHEL : You're not going to tell me?

STRONG :No.

(*Mrs. Loving dressed for the street comes in*)

MRS. LOVING : Goodbye, children. Rachel, don't quarrel so much with John. Let me see—if I have my key. (*Feels in her bag*) Yes, I have it. I'll be back shortly. Good-bye. (*Strong and Rachel rise. He bows*).

RACHEL: Good-bye, Ma dear. Hurry back as soon as you can, won't you? (*Exit Mrs. Loving through the vestibule. Strong leans back again in his chair, and watches Rachel through half-closed eyes. Rachel sits in her chair nervously*).

STRONG: Do you mind, if I smoke?

RACHEL: You know I don't.

STRONG: I am trying to behave like—Reginald—"the properly reared young gentleman caller." (*Lights a cigar; goes over to the fire, and throws his match away. Rachel goes into the kitchenette, and brings him a saucer for his ashes. She places it on the table near him*). Thank you. (*They both sit again, Strong very evidently enjoying his cigar and Rachel*). Now this is what I call cosy.

RACHEL: Cosy! Why?

STRONG: A nice warm room—shut in—curtains drawn—a cheerful fire crackling at my back—a lamp, not an electric or gas one, but one of your plain, old-fashioned kerosene ones—

RACHEL (*Interupting*): Ma dear would like to catch you, I am sure, talking about *her* lamp like that. "Old-fashioned! plain!"—You have nerve.

STRONG (*Continuing as though he had not been interrupted*): A comfortable chair—a good cigar—and not very far away, a little lady, who is looking charming, so near, that if I reached over, I could touch her. You there —and I here.—It's living.

RACHEL: Well! of all things! A compliment—and from *you*! How did it slip out, pray? (*No answer*). I suppose that you realize that a conversation between two persons is absolutely impossible, if one has to do her share all alone. Soon my ingenuity for introducing interesting subjects will be exhausted; and then will follow what, I believe, the story books call, "an uncomfortable silence."

STRONG (*Slowly*): Silence—between friends—isn't such a bad thing.

RACHEL: Thanks awfully. (*Leans back; cups her cheek in her hand, and makes no pretense at further conversation. The old look of introspection returns to her eyes. She does not move*).

STRONG (*Quietly*): Rachel! (*Rachel starts perceptibly*) You must remember I'm here. I don't like looking into your soul—when you forget you're not alone.

RACHEL: I hadn't forgotten.

STRONG: Wouldn't it be easier for you, little girl, if you could tell—some one?

RACHEL: No. (*A silence*)

STRONG: Rachel,—you're fond of flowers,—aren't you?

RACHEL: Yes.

STRONG: Rosebuds—red rosebuds—particularly?

RACHEL (*Nervously*): Yes.

STRONG: Did you—dislike—the giver?

RACHEL (*More nervously; bracing herself*): No, of course not.

STRONG: Rachel,—why—why—did you—kill the roses—then?

RACHEL (*Twisting her hands*): Oh, John! I'm so sorry, Ma dear told you that. She didn't know, you sent them.

STRONG: So I gathered. (*Pauses and then leans forward; quietly*). Rachel, little girl, why—did you kill them?

RACHEL (*Breathing quickly*): Don't you believe—it—a—a —kindness—sometimes—to kill?

STRONG (*After a pause*): You—considered—it—a—kindness—to kill them?

RACHEL: Yes. (*Another pause*)

STRONG: Do you mean—just—the roses?

RACHEL (*Breathing more quickly*): John!—Oh! must I say?

STRONG: Yes, little Rachel.

RACHEL (*In a whisper*): No. (*There is a long pause. Rachel leans back limply, and closes her eyes. Presently Strong rises, and moves his chair very close to hers. She does not stir. He puts his cigar on the saucer*).

STRONG (*Leaning forward; very gently*): Little girl, little girl, can't you tell me why?

RACHEL (*Wearily*): I can't.—It hurts—too much—to talk about it yet,—please.

STRONG (*Takes her hand; looks at it a few minutes and then at her quietly*). You—don't—care, then? (*She winces*) Rachel!—Look at me, little girl! (*As if against her will, she looks at him. Her eyes are fearful, hunted. She tries to look away, to draw away her hand; but he holds her gaze and her hand steadily*). Do you?

RACHEL (*Almost sobbing*): John! John! don't ask me. You are drawing my very soul out of my body with your eyes. You must not talk this way. You mustn't look— John, don't! (*Tries to shield her eyes*).

STRONG (*Quietly takes both of her hands, and kisses the backs and the palms slowly. A look of horror creeps into her face. He deliberately raises his eyes and looks at her mouth. She recoils as though she expected him to strike her. He resumes slowly*) If—you—do—care, and I know now—that you do—nothing else, *nothing* should count.

RACHEL (*Wrenching herself from his grasp and rising. She covers her ears; she breathes rapidly*): No! No! No!— You *must* stop. (*Laughs nervously; continues feverishly*) I'm not behaving very well as a hostess, am I? Let's see. What shall I do? I'll play you something, John. How will that do? Or I'll sing to you. You used to like to hear me sing; you said my voice, I remember, was sympathetic, didn't you? (*Moves quickly to the piano*). I'll sing you a pretty little song. I think it's beautiful. You've never heard it, I know. I've never sung it to you before. It's Nevin's "At Twilight." (*Pauses, looks down, before she begins, then turns toward him and says quietly and sweetly*) Sometimes—in the coming years—I want—you to remember—I sang you this little song.— Will you?—I think it will make it easier for me— when I —when I— (*Breaks off and begins the first chords. Strong goes slowly to the piano. He leans there watching intently. Rachel sings*):

"The roses of yester-year
    Were all of the white and red;
It fills my heart with silent fear
    To find all their beauty fled.

The roses of white are sere,
    All faded the roses red,
And one who loves me is not here
And one that I love is dead."

(*A long pause. Then Strong goes to her and lifts her from the piano-stool. He puts one arm around her very tenderly and pushes her head back so he can look into her eyes. She shuts them, but is passive*).

STRONG (*Gently*): Little girl, little girl, don't you know that suggestions—suggestions—like those you are sending yourself constantly—are wicked things? You, who are so gentle, so loving, so warm—(*Breaks off and crushes her to him. He kisses her many times. She does not resist, but in the midst of his caresses she breaks suddenly into convulsive laughter. He tries to hush the terrible sound with his mouth; then brokenly*) Little girl—don't laugh—like that.

RACHEL (*Interrupted throughout by her laughter*): I have to.—God is laughing.—We're his puppets.—He pulls the wires,—and we're so funny to Him.—I'm laughing too—because I can hear—my little children—weeping. They come to me generally while I'm asleep,—but I can hear them now.—They've begged me—do you understand?—begged me—not to bring them here;—and I've promised them—not to.—I've promised. I can't stand the sound of their crying.—I have to laugh—Oh! John! laugh!—laugh too!—I can't drown their weeping.

(*Strong picks her up bodily and carries her to the arm-chair*).

STRONG (*Harshly*): Now, stop that!

RACHEL (*In sheer surprise*): W-h-a-t?

STRONG (*Still harshly*): Stop that!—You've lost your self-control.—Find yourself again!

(*He leaves her and goes over to the fireplace, and stands looking down into it for some little time. Rachel, little by little, becomes calmer. Strong returns and sits beside her again. She doesn't move. He smoothes her hair back gently, and kisses her forehead—and then, slowly, her mouth. She does not resist; simply sits there, with shut eyes, inert, limp*).

STRONG: Rachel!—(*Pauses*). There is a little flat on 43rd Street. It faces south and overlooks a little park. Do you remember it?—it's on the top floor?—Once I remember your saying—you liked it. That was over a year ago. That same day—I rented it. I've never lived there. No one knows about it—not even my mother. It's completely furnished now—and waiting—do you know for whom? Every single thing in it, I've bought myself—even to the pins on the little bird's-eye maple dresser. It has been

the happiest year I have ever known. I furnished it—
one room at a time. It's the prettiest, the most homelike
little flat I've ever seen. (*Very low*) Everything there—
breathes love. Do you know for whom it is waiting? On
the sitting-room floor is a beautiful, Turkish rug—red, and
blue and gold. It's soft—and rich—and do you know for
whose little feet it is waiting? There are delicate curtains
at the windows and a bookcase full of friendly, eager,
little books.—Do you know for whom they are waiting?
There are comfortable leather chairs, just the right size,
and a beautiful piano—that I leave open—sometimes, and
lovely pictures of Madonnas. Do you know for whom
they are waiting? There is an open fireplace with logs
of wood, all carefully piled on gleaming andirons—and
waiting. There is a bellows and a pair of shining tongs—
waiting. And in the kitchenette painted blue and white,
and smelling sweet with paint is everything: bright pots
and pans and kettles, and blue and white enamel-ware,
and all kinds of knives and forks and spoons—and on the
door—a roller-towel. Little girl, do you know for whom
they are all waiting? And somewhere—there's a big,
strong man—with broad shoulders. And he's willing and
anxious to do anything—everything, and he's waiting very
patiently. Little girl, is it to be—yes or no?

RACHEL (*During Strong's speech life has come flooding
back to her. Her eyes are shining; her face, eager. For
a moment she is beautifully happy*). Oh! you're too good
to me and mine, John. I—didn't dream any one—could
be—so good. (*Leans forward and puts his big hand
against her cheek and kisses it shyly*).

STRONG (*Quietly*) : Is it—yes—or no, little girl?

RACHEL (*Feverishly, gripping his hands*) : Oh, yes! yes!
yes! and take me quickly, John. Take me before I can
think any more. You mustn't let me think, John. And

you'll be good to me, won't you? Every second of every minute, of every hour, of every day, you'll have me in your thoughts, won't you? And you'll be with me every minute that you can? And, John, John!—you'll keep away the weeping of my little children. You won't let me hear it, will you? You'll make me forget everything everything—won't you?—Life is so short, John. (*Shivers and then fearfully and slowly*) And eternity so—long. (*Feverishly again*) And, John, after I am dead—promise me, promise me you'll love me more. (*Shivers again*). I'll need love then. Oh! I'll need it. (*Suddenly there comes to their ears the sound of a child's weeping. It is monotonous, hopeless, terribly afraid. Rachel recoils*). Oh! John!—Listen!—It's my boy, again.—I—John—I'll be back in a little while. (*Goes swiftly to the door in the rear, pauses and looks back. The weeping continues. Her eyes are tragic. Slowly she kisses her hand to him and disappears. John stands where she has left him looking down. The weeping stops. Presently Rachel appears in the doorway. She is haggard, and grey. She does not enter the room. She speaks as one dead might speak—tonelessly, slowly*).

RACHEL: Do you wish to know why Jimmy is crying?

STRONG: Yes.

RACHEL: I am twenty-two—and I'm old; you're thirty-two —and you're old; Tom's twenty-three—and he is old. Ma dear's sixty—and she said once she is much older than that. She is. We are all blighted; we are all accursed— all of us—, everywhere, we whose skins are dark—our lives blasted by the white man's prejudice. (*Pauses*) And my little Jimmy—seven years old, that's all—is blighted too. In a year or two, at best, he will be made old by suffering. (*Pauses*): One week ago, today, some white boys, older and larger than my little Jimmy, as he was leaving the school—called him "Nigger"! They chased him through the streets calling him, "Nigger! Nigger! Nigger!" One boy threw stones at him. There is still a bruise on his little back where one struck him. That will get well; but they bruised his soul—and that— will never—get well. He asked me what "Nigger" meant. I made light of the whole thing, laughed it off. He went to his little playmates, and very naturally asked them. The oldest of them is nine!—and they knew, poor little things—and they told him. *(Pauses)*. For the last couple of nights he has been dreaming—about these boys. And he always awakes—in the dark— afraid—afraid—of the now—and the future—I have seen that look of deadly fear—in the eyes—of other little children. I know what it is myself.—I was twelve— when some big boys chased me and called me names.—I never left the house afterwards—without being afraid. I was afraid, in the streets—in the school—in the church, everywhere, always, afraid of being hurt. And I—was not—afraid in vain. *(The weeping begins again)*. He's only a baby—and he's blighted. *(To Jimmy)* Honey, I'm right here. I'm coming in just a minute. Don't cry. *(To Strong)* If it nearly kills me to hear my Jimmy's crying, do you think I could stand it, when my own child, flesh of my flesh, blood of my blood—learned the same reason for weeping? Do you? *(Pauses)*. Ever since I fell here—a week ago—I am afraid—to go—to sleep, for every time I do—my children come—and beg me— weeping—not to—bring them here—to suffer. Tonight, they came—when I was awake. *(Pauses)*. I have promised them again, now—by Jimmy's bed. *(In a whisper)* I have damned—my soul to all eternity—if I do. *(To Jimmy)* Honey, don't! I'm coming. *(To Strong)* And John,—dear John—you see—it can never be—all the beautiful, beautiful things—you have—told me about. (*Wistfully*) No—they—can never be—now. (*Strong comes toward her*) No,—John dear,—you—must not— touch me—any more. (*Pauses*). Dear, this—is— "Good-bye."

STRONG (*Quietly*): It's not fair—to you, Rachel, to take you—at your word—tonight. You're sick; you've brooded so long, so continuously,—you've lost—your perspective. Don't answer, yet. Think it over for another week and I'll come back.

RACHEL (*Wearily*): No,—I can't think—any more.

STRONG: You realize—fully—you're sending me—for always?

RACHEL: Yes.

STRONG: And you care?

RACHEL: Yes.

STRONG: It's settled, then for all time—"Good-bye!"

RACHEL (*After a pause*): Yes.

STRONG (*Stands looking at her steadily a long time, and then moves to the door and turns, facing her; with infinite tenderness*): Good-bye, dear, little Rachel—God bless you.

RACHEL: Good-bye, John! (*Strong goes out. A door opens and shuts. There is finality in the sound. The weeping continues. Suddenly; with a great cry*) John! John! (*Runs out into the vestibule. She presently returns. She is calm again. Slowly*) No! No! John. Not for us. (*A pause; with infinite yearning*) Oh! John,— if it only—if it only— (*Breaks off, controls herself. Slowly again; thoughtfully*) No—No sunshine—no laughter—always, always—darkness. That is it. Even our little flat— (*In a whisper*) John's and mine—the little flat —that calls, calls us—through darkness. It shall wait— and wait—in vain—in darkness. Oh, John! (*Pauses*). And my little children! my little children! (*The weep-*

ing ceases; pauses). I shall never—see—you—now. Your little, brown, beautiful bodies—I shall never see.— Your dimples—everywhere—your laughter—your tears— the beautiful, lovely feel of you here. (*Puts her hands against her heart*). Never—never—to be. (*A pause, fiercely*) But you are somewhere—and wherever you are you are mine! You are mine! All of you! Every bit of you! Even God can't take you away. (*A pause; very sweetly; pathetically*) Little children!—My little children!—No more need you come to me—weeping—weeping. You may be happy now—you are safe. Little weeping, voices, hush! hush! (*The weeping begins again. To Jimmy, her whole soul in her voice*) Jimmy! My little Jimmy! Honey! I'm coming.—Ma Rachel loves you so. (*Sobs and goes blindly, unsteadily to the rear doorway; she leans her head there one second against the door; and then stumbles through and disappears. The light in the lamp flickers and goes out...It is black. The terrible, heart-breaking weeping continues*).

THE END